RELIGIOUS
PIED PIPERS
PIED PIPERS
PIED PIPERS
PIED PIPERS

RELIGIOUS PIED PIPERS PIED PIPERS PIED PIPERS PIED PIPERS

A Critique of Radical Right-Wing Religion

JOHN CHARLES COOPER

Judson Press® Valley Forge

RELIGIOUS PIED PIPERS

Library of Congress Cataloging in Publication Data

Cooper, John Charles.
  Religious pied pipers.

  Includes bibliographical references.
    1. Evangelicalism—United States—Controversial literature. 2.
Conservatism—United States—History—20th century. 3. United
States—Moral conditions. 4. United States—Church history—20th
century.
I. Title.
BR1642.U5C675   277.3   81-11771
ISBN 0-8170-0907-8   AACR2

Brethren, my heart's desire and prayer to God for them is that they may be saved. I bear them witness that they have a zeal for God, but it is not enlightened (Romans 10:1-2).

Contents

Introduction

Martin Marty, respected church historian, social commentator, and associate editor of *The Christian Century*, annually asks readers and persons contributing articles and reviews to *The Christian Century* to suggest ideas for books that *should be* written. In the May 21, 1980, issue, the Reverend Peter L. Steinke, Hope Lutheran Church, Friendswood, Texas, expressed a need for a book which would deal with "zeal, fanaticism, single-vision forever, either/or mentality, etc., from [a] historical and biblical perspective." Undoubtedly, many other concerned Christians, clergy and lay, faced with the rapidly growing radical "conservatism" of today, have felt the need also for some classification and direction. While possessing no wisdom but the self-confessed ignorance of Socrates and the foolishness for Christ of Paul, the author hopes the present work will fill some of that felt need.

Some years ago, my own infatuation with knowing all the answers received a severe—and saving—jolt when my wife gave me a little sign for my desk. The sign reads, "Education is man's going forward from cocksure ignorance to thoughtful uncertainty." What the sign says of education might be equally well said of Christian faith. We are not given all the answers at our baptism. Omniscience is not one of the gifts of the Spirit bestowed when we are born again. The Bible is surely the Word of God, but it is interpreted—and misinterpreted—over and over again by human beings. As Paul observes, "Now we see in a mirror dimly, but then face to face. Now I know in part; then I shall understand fully, even as I have been fully understood"

RELIGIOUS PIED PIPERS

(1 Corinthians 13:12). Here in the confused and confusing world of politics, social customs, rising expectations, environmental crises, and international conflict, we see the real problems only dimly and understand possible solutions only in part. Lacking certainty, we are thrust back upon the only certainties that endure: faith, hope, and love.

In opposition to the prostitution of that faith, the falsification of that hope, and the denial of that love—all done in the Lord's name—this book is written. The religious Pied Pipers, who now go beyond telling us what is wrong with our society and tell us who to vote for, must be opposed in the name of freedom and of the gospel. The right-wing vision of America represents a corruption of the faith, hope, and love that undergird the Christian community and, to a degree, every human community. We say of the contemporary radical rightists what Paul said of the Pharisees of his day: ". . . they have a zeal for God, but it is not enlightened" (Romans 10:2). Unenlightened zeal is dangerous to the physical, mental, and spiritual lives of God's people. The church cannot be silent when error is trumpeted, for silence in such a case is implied consent. The martyrs of the Christian churches of Germany during World War II have taught us that faith demands a loving but firm and crystal-clear response. "Brethren, do not be children in your thinking; be babes in evil, but in thinking be mature" (1 Corinthians 14:20).

After all is said, this response really is just that—a call not for a zeal which lashes out in all directions, but for the maturity of thinking that characterizes faith seeking understanding.

John Charles Cooper
Winebrenner Theological Seminary
Findlay, Ohio
Spring, 1981

1

The Present Age

Religion once ruled the world. In the Middle Ages the Roman pope claimed the right to confirm or depose kings—and his power was proved in the snow outside his castle at Canossa. The Holy Roman Emperor, Henry IV, bareheaded and barefoot, bowed before the triple crown that represented, to the people of Europe at that time, power on earth granted by the power of heaven. In China the bureaucrat Confucius, laying down the rules for court etiquette and civil service practice, was in time transformed by tradition into the guide of life for half a billion human beings. In India the great King Asoka embraced the teachings of the gentle Buddha, and Buddhism spread to guide the daily lives of millions to this day. Among the Hebrews, prophets confronted kings and priests and pronounced on the values of human life in community. The priests of Egypt, enraged by the monotheism of Ikhnaton, secured the Pharaoh's removal and sought to obliterate his name from the memory of the human race. The authority of religion may be taken lightly by some in the twentieth century, but religion's hold over the minds of hundreds of millions today should not be overlooked. In the brief millennia since the recording of history, perhaps more people have died for religion than for empire or nationalism.

Religion has authority—and rightly so. Some forms of religion, however, seem to foster the dependence of persons upon religious leaders much more than others. In our day, in our place, religious authoritarianism has again begun to flower. It has sprung up on the right side of the theological spectrum, among the Fundamentalists who now claim the name of *Evangelicals*. Surely this claim is a surprise to those conservative Christians who stand in the line of Luther, Calvin, Wesley, and Roger Williams.

Contemporary religious authoritarians disguise their lust for power under the folksy, Appalachian coloration of the "old-time religion." Wearing three-piece suits, sometimes singing to the strumming of guitars, these largely self-educated and self-elected leaders preach a message made of one-third "blood of the cross" evangelism and two-thirds extremist politics. Showing precious little love for sinful humanity and no tolerance for anyone unlike themselves, these leaders denounce the nation, the previous Carter administration, and the manners, morals, and beliefs of almost everyone in America.

Such tirades are ignored by those with a grounding in logic and some knowledge of the world political situation but are absorbed as gospel truth by increasing numbers of people. The anti-Communist, anticontemporary life-style message is adopted by demagogues precisely because it is already an article of faith among many people in the Appalachian mountain region, the South, and the Midwest. And the message is spread throughout North America, planted there by the preaching and music of several generations of radio evangelists and Nashville musicians. This nativist, Know-Nothing message is valuable as a tool for achieving wealth and power, as numerous politicians and independent preachers (sometimes the same persons) have discovered. Religious authority, enhanced by prestige bestowed by media exposure, becomes a basis for power: the power of fame, wealth, and privilege.

Concerned citizens have much to fear from this most recent explosion of thunder on the Right. Christians in particular should be moved to investigate and to counter the efforts of Fundamentalist absolutists. Some in this camp have in the past served as chaplains for Ku Klux Klan Klaverans, denounced school integration, and still teach the inferiority of the black race to the white. The list of intolerance and discrimination of such people is long. There is a reason, going back to May 17, 1954, why this type of religionist dislikes the federal government. Interestingly, one of the suggestions made to combat communism is to stop busing children to integrate the schools!

Everyone with leadership ability, inherent or learned, knows that you can really only lead people where they want to go. You have to get "the sense of the group"; then stay out in front of the crowd when they start to move. Men and women who want power, who are serving themselves rather than working for principle, know that power is awarded to "leaders" who say what the crowd wants to hear. Do the common people feel that America is weak no matter what the president says? Then trump up some figures to "prove" America is weak and cry out for billions of dollars more for defense. (That such a call seems strange from a "minister of the gospel" never seems to cross the Fundamentalist mind.) Do lower-class whites fear economic competition from the blacks? Then denounce integration programs. (Never mind that racial discrimination is unchristian.) Do blue-collar and white-collar workers feel pinched by taxes? Do they feel that "welfare" recipients are the cause of this financial pain? Then denounce welfare programs. (Not that some welfare bureaucracies don't need reform!) These leaders overlook the call of Judeo-Christianity to care for the poor. Do rural and small-town people fear the pluralism of cultures and the wide range of life-styles that flourish in the great cities? Then denounce the cities and the feminists, the gays, the "liberals"—and stand back to reap the rewards of fame and money. The formula is old: as old as the Sophists of Greece, the witch-hunters of New England, and the Know-Nothings of the nineteenth century. The technique is stereotyped; but the more things change, the more the natural instincts of the human heart remain the same.

To some degree, the charges of the demagogues are right. They cry out that there is an absence of leadership in America. They claim that Americans are an aimless, morale-damaged people. It seems fair to say that people seeking the path to power by demagoguery are possible only in a vacuum of clear and strong leadership. Joseph McCarthy appeared under Eisenhower; Billy James Hargis prospered in the same era, and we saw the present onslaught arise under Jimmy Carter. When the gods depart, the half-gods arrive.

Turning Right

For several years religious and political commentators have pointed out the obvious to us: America, in general, is moving toward a more conservative intellectual stance than that which characterized the volatile decade of the 1960s. Utterly weary of the turmoil and experimentation of life-style that the era of the hippies, student confrontations, drugs, and Vietnam conflict brought on, a psychically exhausted populace drew back, looking to the old verities for comfort and rest. The resurfacing of conservatism in mainstream American Protestantism and the ascension to new respectability of old-line Fundamentalism is documented by students of the religious scene, ranging from Dean Kelley of the National Council of Churches to Martin Marty to *Time* magazine's religious editors. If anyone has any doubt that the old-time religion is growing more powerful year by year, a few hours spent before the television set will resolve the question. From all quarters, very conservative, even revivalistic preachers hold forth on both commercial and a growing number of religious stations. Commentators, lumping together such widely different religious groups as the Lutheran Church-Missouri Synod and the independent churches stemming from the Moody Bible Institute, proclaimed the 1970s the decade of the Evangelicals. While a serious study of the phenomenon called "Evangelicalism" would drastically raise questions about both its supposed unity and its claimed number of adherents (sometimes put at fifty million), the 1970s—and the early 1980s—are certainly years of religious conservatism.

Beyond the Protestant scene, the Roman Catholic communion also witnessed some conservative reactions to the recently vocal liberal voices in her midst. Both Pope Paul VI and Pope John Paul II have voiced warnings that not everything has changed in Rome since Vatican II. John Paul's refusal to consider the possibility of women as priests or to modify the church's teaching on birth control and abortion during his triumphant tour of the United States was a firm restatement of the conservative stance now taken in the vastly reformed Roman Catholic Church.

As the pendulum of thought, experience, and acceptance ran leftward toward ever more liberal possibilities in the 1960s, in the 1970s and early 1980s the pendulum has swung more and more toward the Right.

The problem does not lie in the move to the Right. Conservatism is one possible way of looking at life. *It is not conservatism, but actually radicalism masquerading as conservatism* that now deforms the present religious and social situation in America. To understand this state of affairs, we must go beyond news reports and claims and counterclaims and, like Socrates, examine the language and evidence of the zealous ones who speak so loudly today.

It is instructive to examine the arguments advanced for the turn Right[1] in religious thinking today. We are told that people are looking for security and something solid to believe in. The relief of anxiety given by the end of World War II was followed by the depressing advent of the cold war within two years. The conflicts of the fifties in Korea and in what was then Indochina left Americans sick of war. The sixties dawned, for many youngsters, as the "Age of Aquarius,"[2] a time of romantic longing for peace. This peace was not to be. Along with the "laid back" life-style of pot smokers, the smoldering embers of race conflict blew into flame. Assassinations of political and religious leaders from Malcom X to John F. Kennedy, from Bobby Kennedy to Martin Luther King, Jr., brought on an age of confrontation, both over race relations and over the Southeast Asian war. This conflict somehow expanded, like the spirits from Pandora's box, without our being aware of it.

Nostalgia As Politics and Theology

In his pre-World War II novel, *It Can't Happen Here,*[3] Sinclair Lewis portrays an America under the grip of a native American fascism, whose symbol is not the swastika but the Rotary wheel. Lewis's acute analysis is based on the insight that fascism builds itself on the middle-class values held to by the "haves" in any society. Political absolutism takes control through the manipulation of beliefs and symbols that are dear to the average man and woman. "The fifth column" is the enemy within the gates who steals our liberty by claiming to defend the very values of decency and lawful order it secretly despises. Above all, fascism portrays itself as patriotism, showing that patriotism (while noble in its genuine expression) is often the last resort of scoundrels. Militant, politically oriented Fundamentalism sounds dangerously familiar. Hitler, too, denounced the elements of German society that he claimed were perverting Nordic morality—Jews, Gypsys, artists, writers, Communists. We too often forget that Nazism began as an anti-Communist crusade.[4]

Considering the dangers that loose religiously patriotic talk can bring, we might paraphrase Ludwig Wittgenstein's famous dictum,

15

"Philosophy is often the disease of which it should be the cure," by saying, "Religion is often the sin of which it should be the cure." Pure religion and undefiled is to show mercy and compassion on others and to live ethical lives (see James 1:27). The popular (one almost says "cultic") religion of the mass media evangelists turns out, upon examination, to be a projection of anger and frustration and often of race hatred and class dislike. The contemporary world (for us, say the United States since 1945) has been an exhilarating experience for some people; for most it has been strange, unpredictable, and unsettling. Somehow the triumphs of climbing upward in social class and moving outward to ever-greener suburbs have been spoiled by those "other people" who keep insisting on rights and some upward mobility of their own. Try as hard as we may, many of us lose our tempers when we think of blacks, Chicanos, feminists, gays, and hippies. Compassion and forgiveness go out the window when we feel threatened in our status and possessions. The mass media evangelists know that we, the middle classes, have reached this point of psychic fatigue. But rather than trying to heal us and help us to a positive, forgiving attitude, these Fundamentalists have ground the anger and frustration even deeper into people's minds and feelings. Such preaching is religiously cancerous.

When elderly people begin to talk of the "good old days" (these days they mean "before television" rather than "before the automobile"!), we smile tolerantly. Everything looks better from the distance of some decades. The rough places become smooth from the perspective of the years. But nostalgia ceases to be tolerable when it becomes a demonic myth, just as the admiration of tall, blue-eyed blondes ceases to be tolerable when it becomes demonic racism. What we note in the writings and speeches of Fundamentalist religionists and ultraconservative political speakers is just such a demonic distortion of the myth of America's past.[5] Interestingly, many Americans respond with fervor to the grade school level recounting of America's "pure" foundation and past. Even the events of quite recent history can be redefined and made pure by the arch-conservative. Witness Ronald Reagan's declaration before the 1980 American Legion convention that the Vietnam War was "good." His remarks were happily received.

Others have gone into detail exploding the myth of America's "pure" past, and I have covered the subject in my book *The Recovery of America*. "Revisionist" historians have finally put in print the long story of treachery and murder practiced against the "Indians" in the conquest and settlement of this land. America is great and it may be good, but it hardly was produced by a virgin birth!

Of course, the nostalgia for a lost, pure past is much older than America. This belief that, somehow, the good days all lie behind us in the distant past, "once upon a time," is the foundation of the appeal of the Garden of Eden story. Myths far older than the Hebrew Scriptures convey this longing. Basically, nostalgia for a perfect past now lost is a pessimistic world view. "Nothing now can come to any good" might be a good motto for premillennialist doom-saying. This world is infected by evil, in this view, and everything here must go smash before God creates "a new heaven and a new earth"—i.e., *restores* the original Garden of Eden in all its pristine purity.

Much Fundamentalism is unconscious of the mythic quality of its philosophy and of its similarity to philosophies in non-Christian religions and in heretical cults. Very many Fundamentalists are simple "biblical literalists" because they have a low threshold for the anxiety caused by paradoxical, ambiguous situations. These people are made very insecure by the possibility that morality may demand different actions in different contexts or that biblical texts may be interpreted in different ways. They long for the simple—and seemingly clear—interpretations and authority of the Bible as it was taught to them in Sunday school. Many Fundamentalists seem to be adults who have not grown beyond the youngster's literal level of theology.

All this would be fine if it were limited to a person's personal life. There is a problem, however, when such an outlook is imposed upon national and international affairs. The disturbances such a literalistic, revisionist religio-political outlook can cause a society is graphically seen in the recent events in Iran. Seeing the problems caused when *someone* (or something, in the Fundamentalist Islamic and Protestant Christian contexts, specifically, a book) is made absolute and infallible in a complex political situation should give a thinking person pause. One begins to understand the uneasy feeling the religious and secular leaders of Judea felt in the presence of

Jesus Christ. Of course, the leaders of Judea didn't take Jesus' own dictum, "Render unto Caesar the things that are Caesar's and unto God the things that are God's," seriously. *Jesus himself rejected the concept of theocracy* and pointed to the doctrine of the two kingdoms later developed by Augustine and refined in the early Reformation period by Martin Luther. To render unto Caesar his due and yet not to neglect the spiritual realm is divine counsel to live with the separation of the church and state. Paradoxically, those who claim to take the Bible literally and some even to stand in the Free Church, Baptist tradition, are attacking the separation of church and state. The Moral Majority and other religious critics of American politics are guilty of running roughshod over the wall of separation. These critics have gone beyond the moral criticism of the state that is the church's traditional duty to a stance of threatening the state—and even, it seems, of planning to take it over—all in the name of the Lord.

Declaring belief in the separation of church and state and devotion to freedom and spiritual interests, the right-wing Fundamentalists boldly interfere in the political process in an authoritarian manner. Harry and Bonaro Overstreet have precisely defined the character of extremists in their classic work, *The Strange Tactics of Extremism.*[6] Such personalities reject any kind of authority over them (such as government) but wish to exercise dictatorial authority over others. Cultural pluralism, true social freedom, they despise.

An old Roman proverb says, "Distrust that man in whom the urge to punish is strong." On that ground alone we may identify the authoritarians among us. The vehemence with which people, programs, and problems are denounced by so-called Evanglicals in politics shows the anger, the urge to punish in them. Denouncing homosexuals, people with other life-styles, the poor on welfare, and above all, Communist sympathizers, the burden of the Moral Majority message is punitive against every category of person that doesn't fit the evangelists' mold. The narrow-minded selfishness of such a position is self-evident, as is a lust for power—power to make others conform to one's image of what is right. The riches that such a role can and does bring need not be belabored. The only real question is: why do so many relatively powerless, not wealthy people, respond to the religious authoritarian message? It isn't the leaders but the followers who present problems in interpretation. The desire to acquire the respect and prestige that success usually gives the popular and wealthy in America certainly seems to motivate some of the now politically oriented evangelists. The Reverend James Robison, speaking of a Dallas meeting of Fundamentalists with Ronald Reagan, observed: "This one meeting could easily turn out an extra 5 million, perhaps 10 million, voters. That should quiet those who ridicule us."[7] The prestige that having millions of followers gives to main-line denominational heads has never been granted the Fundamentalist evangelists, and, like the newly rich in every era, this must gall them. Famous professors and outstanding divinity schools (not to mention the general run of theological seminaries) simply do not accept these self-made prophets, not even when the mass media gives them front-page coverage. That situation explains in part the animosity these "leaders" show toward "liberal" professors—and their general anti-intellectualism. The aura of respectability refused the evangelists by divinity schools and churches is sought through influencing national politics. In a national mood of polemicism toward the Equal Rights Amendment, feminism, abortion, homosexuality, and welfare programs, the evangelists seem to have found their chance to vie for power.

But in America—as everywhere else in the world—money, finally, is power. The radio-television evangelists are also charging that the federal government, through the Federal Communications Commission and the Internal Revenue Service, are interfering with the separation of church and state. By this they mean that some accountability for the huge revenues they take in is being suggested. A lot of the turnaround from the traditional Fundamentalist quietism, or "hands-off politics" view, seems to be caused by a desire to protect the money-making operations that the evangelists have created. Religious broadcasting is a big business in America. It is estimated that 1,300 radio and thirty-six television stations devote all or most of their time to religion.[8] Gospel programs that get free time or buy time on commercial stations also are growing. The money is rolling in. Jerry Falwell collects $50 million a year. Oral Roberts has built a $200 million "City of Faith" at Tulsa. Pat Robertson has parlayed the *700 Club* into an international headquarters and television network at Virginia Beach, Virginia.

RELIGIOUS PIED PIPERS

These people want to protect their incomes. Only the Federal Communications Commission and the Internal Revenue Service represent a possible check on their unregulated use of the publicly owned airways and of the publicly contributed millions of dollars. We may well think the evangelists protest too much.

The Right-Wing Religious Groups

There are at least four national movements that attempt to influence American politics with right-wing, ultraconservative religious views. These are Christian Voice, directed by Richard Zone; Moral Majority, founded by Jerry Falwell; the Religious Roundtable, headed by Edward McAteer, and the National Christian Action Coalition, a kind of behind-the-scenes brain trust that works for the other groups. Just as in radical rightist politics, the same names keep cropping up on the platforms and executive boards of all these groups. Falwell speaks for the Religious Roundtable and the other evangelists are quoted by all these groups.

The events in America of the 1960s and early 1970s were radical and novel, to say the least. It was natural that reactions would set in. Nevertheless, the sharp change of mood in American society, called by Gerald R. Gill "the meanness mania,"[9] is *radical* in itself. This changed mood is described as a turning away from support of social and legal programs designed to include more blacks and other minorities (including the white poor) in the benefits of mainstream society. While not necessarily "racist" in every case, such a mood—and action—is selfish. Ironically, we have a so-called Moral Majority advocating selfishness in the name of the old-time religion. Faustine Childress Jones in *The Changing Mood in America: Eroding Commitment?* defines this changed mood:

> The mood is shifting from helping the underprivileged and racial minorities to a great social concern for the middle-income and affluent classes. This change has been camouflaged with euphemistic language, thus making the state of regression less descernible [sic].[10]

Studies reported by Jones indicate that membership in a church, Protestant or Catholic, seems to have little or no influence on white racial attitudes.[11] Indeed, we are reminded of other sociological studies that demonstrate an increasing racial intolerance correlated with commitment to conservative religious groups. Anti-Semitism and Fundamentalist beliefs are shown to be correlated in the studies of Glock and Stark.[12] What is more to the point, there seems to be an affinity between the attraction of very conservative religious views and radically rightist political opinions. Nowhere is this better demonstrated than in the Logos International publication *Reagan in Pursuit of the Presidency—1980*.[13] Interestingly, these Fundamentalist authors go out of their way, by reproducing the transcript of a television interview, to try to show Reagan as a "born-again" Christian. The fact that then President Carter is also a "born-again" Christian seems to count for nothing. Clearly it is not the fact of being "born again" or not "born again" that matters to the religious right, but the *opinions* held by a particular person. The required opinions include opposition to communism, support for capital punishment, support for prayer in public schools, support for a strong national defense, and opposition to gay rights, to the Equal Rights Amendment (ERA), to Salt II, and to abortion. The strange admixture of militarism, discrimination, and legalism about moral issues is typical of the confusion of the Moral Majority movement. This confusion is first of all one of intellect—persons fail to grasp the real issues in our society. It may also be a result of the fact that the "new Right" is not a single organized movement at all. Richard Sennett, writing in *The New York Review of Books* for September 25, 1980, observes that the new Right comprises at least two distinct forces, to which we might add a third, the residual racists in America. Very often white racists have been attracted to the Bible, interpreted in a literalist sense, just as black racists (e.g. the early Black Islamic movements) have been attracted to a literalist reading of the Koran, the holy book of Christianity's historic opponent, Islam. By means of *eisegesis,* reading one's prior beliefs and wishes into the text, racists have come up with "biblical proof" that one race is inferior to another. The cursing of Ham by Noah (Genesis 9:20-27) is the classic proof text for white racists:

> "Cursed be [Ham, the father of] Canaan;
> a slave of slaves shall he be to
> his brothers."
> —Genesis 9:25

The fact that this is a primitive way of justifying the Hebrew

RELIGIOUS PIED PIPERS

(Semite) conquest of the land of Canaan is, of course, completely overlooked by racists.

By the same logic (or lack of it) racists and others obsessed with various fears or beliefs transfer the literal authority they give to a sacred book to a person who expounds their views publicly. A Hitler or an Ayatollah Khomeini can arise. The cult of the book can lead to the cult of personality, but behind both is the desire to legitimatize some belief system that ordinary, civilized society rejects.

Anxiety is Father of All

In 1945 the International Missionary Council published a study, *Religious Liberty: an Inquiry,* by M. Searle Bates, a professor at Nanking University. This lengthy, well-documented work focused on the abuses of religious freedom under the Axis powers and in conservative Roman Catholic countries. Naturally, at that time, attention was fixed on state compulsion and on political oppression. Nevertheless, this document anticipates the form in which religious authoritarianism exists in the 1980s when it warns:

> Political religion is the dangerous foe of true religion.
> The political use of voluntary religion is also inimical to religious liberty.
> Serious issues are raised by the claims of certain religions or religious bodies to control the state, education, culture, or the conscience of the entire community.
> What is the rightful place, in liberty, of religion and religious organizations in the field of general education?[14]

In the 1980s, with private "religious" schools expanding all around us in the Protestant community and with Evangelicals united to make their vision of the Moral Majority the law of the land, these warnings are timely. Reading of the great dangers to religious liberty by right-wing Catholic governments thirty-five years ago gives one a strange feeling when one considers the contemporary religious scene. The very groups that opposed Catholicism and shouted "separation of church and state" for centuries (and still hypocritically shout it) seem determined to erase the wall of separation in favor of their kind of religion controlling the state. Religious oppression is not the monopoly of Catholic countries, as reflection upon the Puritan theocracy in New England and Calvin's Geneva demonstrates.

The opposite of religious authoritarianism is religious liberty. Such liberty has always been a problem in history. Conquerors in ancient times regularly forced the subjugated to acknowledge the conquerors' gods. Throughout the long history of Western expansionism, both Protestant and Catholic missionaries were followed closely by something like the marines. Sometimes, as in the Spanish conquest of America, the two came together. Pluralism, the free exercise of many different religious beliefs, is a system that grew out of long conflict in Great Britain—and it is a particularly valuable portion of the American heritage.

Studying a treatise on religious liberty means learning more about the tyranny exercised over people in the name of religion than a church person can comfortably tolerate. While condemning religious persecution, the loud voices of the Moral Majority sound fanatical—and suggestive of possible future persecution—to sensitive Christians. One can understand religious fanaticism as a possible development under persecution. Having to suffer for the faith can give one a very deep, narrow commitment to it. One wonders what persecution contemporary Evangelicals (if that term is properly applied to them) feel they are suffering? One cannot take too seriously the charges of self-elected revivalists and television personalities that ours is a godless society. Secularism, i.e., pluralism of belief and of no belief, with a separation of church and state, is the result of the desire to give many and varied religious communities full freedom of worship and belief. One can postulate positive goals, not negative responses to persecution, as the reasons for this new tide of religious authoritarianism; there is the desire for conformity, for group solidarity—an illiberal and antidemocratic desire for a society which is religiously, racially, and culturally homogeneous. This is a regression to a pagan and/or medieval form of society and must be resisted in the name of liberty, political as well as religious. Overt as well as covert racial and ethnic (and sexual) prejudicies underlie this general disaffection with the modern temper.

Modern Western adults take it for granted, if they are psychologically healthy, reasonably content socially, individually, and economically, that freedom is the greatest good. Rather than being overwhelmed by the abundance of choices and the many decisions that face them every day, they either rejoice in them or accept them as their due. Deciding between lunch at a kosher deli or a Chinese restaurant, choosing which suit to wear in the morning, whether to drive the car or take a train, and casting a vote for one of several candidates all give life its flavor—for the well adjusted. Being able to control one's impulses, refraining from making advances to an attractive member of the opposite sex, refusing to be drawn into an argument or a fist fight are all part of the possibilities of the psychologically stable. Choosing what to do, when and where, including choosing to go to work or to class or to see a physician seems normal and natural. The cacophony of noise and the panorama of possibilities sometimes weary the normal person, but they never drive the healthy to despair or fear. Even the events and ideas and sights that disturb, that cause anxiety to the well balanced are integrated and handled well psychologically. The decisions to worship, pray, and contribute to churches all fit into this pattern of life for many in our society. Religion is freely chosen and freely followed—for many, for most, but not for all.

For some in American society the supermarket of possibilities and the carnival of events are overwhelming. The free intercourse of all kinds of life-styles, ideas, and communications is deeply disturbing for a growing minority. For these not-well-adjusted ones, a free and open society is frightening, even disgusting. These people want to limit discourse and communication; they want to wall off disturbing life-styles and beliefs. They welcome the coming of an antiseptic environment in which only "safe" ideas and activities are admitted. While they may continue to work in the world, they effectively withdraw psychologically—and to a great extent, socially—from the free society around them. They often identify with Fundamentalist churches. Such folk are ready to give up their freedom with its bewildering choices in order to hear words of comfort and reinforcement—and to be told what to do. These are the many who want—and get—religious authoritarianism. The root cause of their desire is anxiety and unease with our free society and with religion that is incarnated—involved—with that society. The driving force in such people's lives soon becomes religious fanaticism. They undergo religious and social separation—an unwholesome interior removal of themselves from the world and the social processes around them.

Such retreaters from our society form the backbone of the

ultraconservative Protestant congregations around us. They make up a large part of the radio and television audiences that support the "electronic church." We need to understand these people's hurts and move to meet them out of Christian love and compassion. At a time when Roman Catholicism is promoting more and more lay freedoms, it is ironic that extremist Protestants are adopting medieval ways of practicing religion. In effect, those in retreat are creating their own—artificial—worlds, playing at being religious and letting the unchurched go unserved. Powerful personalities, all too willing to tell others what to believe and how to live, have arisen and become famous and wealthy. Others have turned Christianity into nonthreatening entertainment. As Mark R. Sills says in the January 21, 1981, *Christian Century,* these evangelists have created a modern Docetic, heretical form of Christianity.

The roots of religious authoritarianism can be sought in two different directions in modern American society. We can seek first the elements in the religious psyche that are drawn to the absolutist pronouncements of preaching, or we can seek the external processes in our social life that feed on—and foster—the dependency feelings of conservative religious persons. There is both an inner and an outer dimension to the rise of religious fanaticism in our time.

Let's begin here with the external elements and face up to the base elements behind all others: money and power. For it is not just the uncertainties and fears of contemporary life that have brought the ultraconservatives to public prominence today. Those very real fears, uncertainties, and frustrations engage and energize the internal dependence within many of us. Such fears are rather the excuse for the hucksters to press even harder for prime time exposure and those $50 million-a-year contributions television and radio audiences can give.

Even the genuinely conservative journal *Christianity Today* has attacked those who are now "peddling the power and the promises."[15]

Contributing Factors

To discuss the present religious-political situation in America by rehearsing, briefly, the history of the United States since the 1950s may seem strange, but we are where we are now simply because of where we have been. To understand the frustrations, fears, angers, and anxieties of a large part of the American public is impossible unless we understand the real world, hard events that have caused those feelings to surface in everyday people. Since the major events of the past few decades are relatively familar to most people, we only note them here.

Above all, the cold war or confrontation of the United States and its allies with communism, specifically with the Soviet Union and with Red China, plays a major role in the Rightist world view. Since the Berlin Blockade in 1947 and the Korean War of 1950-1953, Americans, or at least a large part of them, have felt threatened and anxious about communism. The development of Soviet atomic weapons later in the same decade raised this anxiety to great heights, leading to such books and movies as *On the Beach* and other "doomsday" scenarios.

Of course, rivalry with the Soviet Union is a fact of life in the second half of the twentieth century. Although there were "Red scares" after World War I and a real dislike of communism, particularly by Christians and conservatives during the twenties and thirties, the Soviet Union itself was not considered a military danger until 1947. World War II brought great devastation to the Soviet Union and its battle with Nazi Germany was won only with the help of the West. In May, 1945, the Allied armies stood supreme in Europe; and while the Red army was huge and powerful, the Western Allies were formidable with the bulk of their strength being the eight-million-man United States Army. Due to the security of our continental location, a two-ocean navy, and the greater destruction visited on both friend and foe by the just-concluded war, the United States stood supreme economically and militarily in the world. We must not forget that suspicion of the Soviet Union was never absent in the West, even when we were allies against Nazi Germany. I do not imply that this suspicion was paranoid or wrong. After all, the Soviet Union had first made allies with the Nazi state in order to conquer the Baltic countries and to divide Poland between Germany and Russia. Russia did not attack Germany, but Hitler foolishly attacked Russia.

Winston Churchill is reported to have had a plan whereby the millions of captured German soldiers would be rearmed and thrown back into battle if the Red army had not stopped at the agreed-on dividing point in Europe between the Russians and the Western Allies. Fear of communism is not new or necessarily unfounded. Then the United States completely demobilized. Within months the huge host of corps and divisions were returned to the United States. Russia did not so demobilize. The military supremacy of the United States as a land-war power disappeared with that demobilization. The belief was that our atomic weapons and huge air force gave us strategic supremacy without a huge army—and this was true for a few years.

When the right wing speaks of the decline of America's power and of the rise of the Soviet Union to parity with the United States and, many say, to Russian strategic as well as tactical superiority over the United States, they are pointing back to this brief moment in time when America was victorious and relatively unhurt by the violence of World War II. There was a short-lived period of euphoria when the world was our oyster. Then the realities of power politics struck us squarely on the nose in the Berlin Blockade. The cold war, sometimes hotter and often cooler, has been the background of everyone's life since 1947.

It should not be surprising, then, that behind so much of the anxiety that the Carter administration could not dispel is this constant fear of the Soviet Union. This explains why moral issues are approached in terms of how abortion or homosexual rights or women's rights threaten the security of the country. But there is also a key to that outlook on life in what scholars call American civil religion. In the minds of American Protestants particularly, living in a nation isolated from the rest of the world in the continental land mass of North America and faced throughout the nineteenth century only by weaker neighbors and tribal societies of native Americans, the deep belief grew up that America was a chosen nation and that its people were God's people. No other country or people had been elected by God to build the perfect society. Part of this belief lay in the nationalistic belief that America is undefeatable. "We have never lost a war," generations of school children were taught—until the Vietnam conflict made that belief untenable. Along the way the millions who believed in the goodness and superiority of America had to struggle with the stalemated war in Korea. The stalemate offended much of the population, and the fact that conservative commentators declared that the conflict could

27

have been won if we had used all our strength laid the basis for wide belief in a conspiracy theory. According to this conspiracy theory, America really *was* the supreme power in the world, and the only way its position could be hurt was by itself, that is, by the betrayal of American interests by some Americans themselves. During the McCarthy era the "Communists" attacked were not the Soviets but Americans. McCarthy rarely mentioned Stalin, surely the most vicious of Communist leaders, but attacked members of the movie industry, writers, and even churchmen. The belief was that America was so great and protected by God that if our rivals had triumphed over us, it could only be because they were aided by other Americans.

Then came the decade and more of involvement in Vietnam. Witnessing the first defeat in 1954—a defeat that many conservative elements wished to prevent by introducing American air strikes to assist the French—military and civilian leaders full of America's sense of superiority gradually took up the battle that France could not win, confidently believing that we could. The rise and fall of the level of the American involvement, the numbers of forces committed, and the size of the casualty rate fluctuated for a decade—leading even to the defeat of administrations and the election of a conservative president because the majority of the American people could not and would not accept the fact that America could be unsuccessful in war. Interestingly, the best military minds held that Korea and Vietnam were the wrong wars in the wrong place at the wrong time. The real enemy and the real strategic threat, these leaders held, was the Soviet Union, not client states or nationalistic rebellions. But the myth of American providential protection was paralleled by the myth of a monolithic international Communist conspiracy. Therefore, attacking liberal college professors in America or left-wing revolutionaries in Southeast Asia was part of one defense of goodness against evil. America would prevail not just because it was strong but because it was good.

Then the blows fell. We did not succeed in Vietnam. The withdrawal from the south, followed immediately by South Vietnam's collapse, was an overwhelming defeat for the military and political policies of several political administrations, both Democratic and Republican. This defeat was so total that it made the stalemate of Korea in 1953—which preserved South Korea as an ally of the West—look like an overwhelming victory. If the result of the Korean War was the casting of doubt on American self-confidence, then the result of Vietnam was a horrible erosion of that self-confidence. But there was more than the sting of defeat, in the military sense, involved. From the standpoint of civil religion—which is the standpoint of the Moral Majority—this looked like abandonment by God. This seemed like a blow not only to national prestige but also to the nation's spiritual status. Why would God allow something like this to happen? What has America done to deserve the withdrawal of the divine favor? A reading of the Old Testament, to the literalist who unqualifiedly reads reference to Israel as a chosen nation as references to America, gives the answer. God had abandoned his Chosen People in the past, not once but on many occasions. In the period of the Judges when the Israelites sinned, God allowed them to be oppressed by their enemies. Only when the people repented did God send a strong man or woman to lead them to triumph over their enemies. But once Israel was free and grew rich, the people would once again fall away from God. In order to bring the Israelites to their senses, God would allow another oppressor to arise and bring them to defeat. This cycle recurs again and again in Judges.

Throughout the period of the kingdom of Israel (and after Solomon's death, of the kingdoms of Israel and Judah) the prophets made clear that the prosperity and freedom of the Chosen People depended on righteousness of life and worship of the true God. It was Solomon's toleration of idolatry in Jerusalem that the biblical historians credited with the breakup up the kingdom in 931 B.C. Before that it was David's adultery with Bathsheba that made him unfit to build God's temple. During the long years of the several royal houses that followed David and Solomon, the righteousness of a king would be followed by prosperity for the nation and safety against all its foes. Whenever the king, the priests, and people sinned, retribution soon followed. Ultimately, idolatry and injustice brought about the destruction of the kingdom of Israel and, later, of the southern kingdom of Judah. God's people would have disappeared from history if he had not preserved to himself a righteous remnant out of which he could fashion, in the future, a more obedient nation who observed his law. This righteous remnant, which arose among the captives carried away to exile in Assyria and Babylonia, had a long history during the time the kingdoms of Israel and Judah existed. A reading of the prophets can identify the righteous remnant as the circles responsive to the denunciations of sin—and interestingly, disdainful of foreign entanglements with Egypt, Syria, and other nations. These prophetic circles denounced not only the worship of false gods but also the wickedness of people's life-styles. The prophets seemed to draw a straight line between personal righteousness, social righteousness, and the security of the state.

Translating from the idiom of the seventh and eighth centuries B.C. into the thought world of the late twentieth century, many conservative religious people saw a direct parallel to the misadventures of Israel and the frightening events of our time. If America was defeated in war, intimidated by an enemy that seemed to grow stronger as America grew weaker, then since Americans are God's chosen people, it can only be because God allows it to happen. God would only do that if America had abandoned God's ways and embraced false beliefs, either beliefs derived from communism or from the idolatry of self-worship, now called "secular humanism."[16] *America is suffering because America has prostituted its spiritual values and is walking in wickedness—this is the undergirding concept of the Moral Majority.* The answer, of course, is that America must repent. Thus, there is a direct relationship between the life-style of the homosexual who flouts the prohibitions attributed to both Moses and Paul, the humanist who does not credit God with the creation of the world, and the feminist who violates Paul's teaching that women should be in subjection to men, and the abandonment of America's enterprises by the God of righteousness and victory. From this perspective, which I believe is basic to all right-wing religious views and, in a secularized version, is basic to conservative political views, we are not engaged in an economic, political, cultural, and military rivalry with the Soviet Union but in a spiritual struggle that is fought out on the moral level. "If you are good, you will succeed; and if you are not good, you will not succeed" is the foundational core of the civil religion. This theme is picked up from the cultural Protestantism widespread in America and organized into a meaningful platform by the Moral Majority.

There is no need to belabor this; the evidence lies in every utterance and writing of the religious Right. The Soviet Union is identified as the Antichrist or in some fashion with Assyria, as the biblical enemy that opposes the people of God. Additionally, much support is gathered from conservative Christians for the state of Israel since in the apocalyptic eschatology of some forms of Fundamentalism the belief is that the end of the world with the battle of Armageddon is soon to come. The existence of the state of Israel and conflict in the Middle East is "proof" of this interpretation of history to such people.

The upshot of all this is that the Moral Majority position *must be militaristic,* for the chosen people must be ready and able to strike down their godless enemies and reverse the debacles brought about by the immorality of many of America's peoples. On the other hand, the Moral Majority position must attack beliefs and life-styles that the Fundamentalist considers sinful since no amount of armament can prevail against the godless enemy as long as America itself is godless and immoral. Only a moral people can recapture the initiative and regain world superiority. It is a strong and stirring message that grabs the imagination of many.

Once more the evidence for the accuracy of this interpretation lies everywhere. There is little said about the Soviet Union except to point to its relative growth in power, *vis à vis* the United States. The real crux of the attack of the religious Right is against other Americans, summed up in a conspiracy theory-type term, "secular humanism." Rather than attacking Soviet slave labor camps, there is an attack on sex education and the teaching of biology in public schools. The immediate as well as long-range agenda of the Moral Majority and other right-wing groups is to make homosexual activity illegal, to make abortions illegal, and to reverse the gains in equality by women and other "minorities," which includes the destruction of the Equal Rights Amendment and perhaps the repeal of the Voting Rights Act of 1964. None of this seems directed toward opposing communism or strengthening the United States militarily. Indeed, it is not, and *the Moral Majority can actually stand against legislation that would strengthen the country's might, such as a new military draft, because it is feared the draft would take women as well as men and thus further institutionalize the equality of women.*

RELIGIOUS PIED PIPERS

The Moral Majority position is an attack on what its leaders have decided is immoral behavior. While they base this reasoning on the civil religion—not the Christian religion—they are more concerned with reversing progressive social reform and eliminating life-styles that disturb them than they are in opposing communism or dealing with real national problems, such as the energy crisis and inflation. Even the civil religion which is hidden behind the Moral Majority's flaunted Christian religion is abandoned in favor of *its foundational interest, the restoration of the privileged place of white, male, middle-class, Christian Americans:* The Moral Majority is a series of boxes within boxes but ultimately is a case of *status politics* wrapped in a sense of moral outrage, which is probably genuine in many people and may be affected by leaders who recognize the political power which that outrage represents.

The idea that we can strengthen the country by strengthening morality is not necessarily wrong. The real question is, "How is morality strengthened?" Certainly nothing that violates human civil liberties and attempts to force people to be "good" strengthens morality. Indeed, as many social commentators have shown, the rigidities of a closed society precisely prevent the development of personal moral responsibility. In all events, we can hardly preserve freedom and democracy by abandoning the rights of the individual to lead his or her own life in his or her own way. To think that we can is to commit the fallacy of utter confusion, symbolized by the artillery captain in Vietnam who reported of a village, "We had to destroy it in order to save it." The result of many of the Moral Majority recommendations, if they were carried out, would be to make the United States more like the Soviet Union and, in fact, prove the conspiracy theory true. We would have destroyed freedom and the opportunity for spiritual and moral growth out of a lack of faith in freedom and morality. We would have opposed the enemy by becoming similar to the authoritarian and oppressive spirit that we rightly fear in communism.

I cannot leave this topic without observing the psychological foolishness of the agenda of both the old Right and the new Right that seeks to—it says—oppose communism by persecuting homosexuals and attacking women's liberation. This is a foolishness that not only neglects the real issues of international competition in our time but also diverts attention and energy away from dealing with world problems. Surely this is a spiritual fifth column in the heart of the nation that weakens us in our struggle to find a peaceful world for ourselves and all nations. It misses the point completely. In the words of Alfred North Whitehead, logically it is a case of "misplaced concretion." This means we have placed the emphasis in the wrong spot and missed the real challenges that confront us.

Finally, trying to defend America and fight communism by attacking the ERA and criticizing the public schools is directly analogous to the worker who is chewed out by his boss on the job and comes home and beats his wife. The essence of the Moral Majority criticism is misdirected aggression. Since the people who make up this movement can do nothing to hurt the Soviets, then it is convenient to find a scapegoat in those persons and movements here at home that disturb us for other reasons.

The tragedy is that neither morality nor politics nor the good of the whole commonwealth is served by any of this. The Christian faith, misrepresented and its commandments misused, suffers again from the judgment of the world that it is irrelevant, reactionary, and based on ignorance. Only the genuine believer knows that despite the prostitution of faith and morals by Christ's overzealous friends, none of those charges is true.

I have no quarrel with those who would bring their Christian faith to bear upon the problems of society and the ambiguities of religious vision as it contemplates political realities. Indeed, the Fundamentalists of the 1976-1980 period are simply acknowledging that their self-chosen opponents, "the liberals," have always been right in insisting that religion should seek to influence social thought and legislation. The problem arises not when religion and politics are brought together, but when a religion that is already a political (i.e. social, earthbound) system is opposed to the legitimate, pluralistic social order made up of believers in many religions. Such absolutist principles and implied hatred of other social visions and life-styles as is shown by the Moral Majority, Christian Voice, Religious Roundtable, and Christian Action Coalition reveal this movement to be a political religion, an expression of the values of a human class growing out of a particular set of historical conditions. While all the new Right organizations do not fit into a neat sociological package, they do largely express the fears and resentments of the middle class living in the Midwest, South, and West. The enemies this movement attacks are the so-called establishment groups and intellectuals of the Northeast. *The politics of this Christian coalition appear to be status politics, a struggle to preserve and enhance the status and power of a group* (or several groups, for the newly wealthy blue-collar class is also involved) *that feels it does not have the influence and respect it deserves.* It emphatically is nothing like the humble service implied in Jurgen Moltmann's vision of political or liberation theology:

> Political hermeneutics calls especially for dialogue with socialist, democratic, humanistic, and anti-racist movements. Political hermeneutics reflects the new situation of God in the inhuman situations of men, in order to break down the hierarchical relationships which deprive them of self-determination, and to help to develop their humanity.[17]

The Moral Majority is not really interested in morality or ethics in the universal sense. There is no Kantian categorical imperative, no sense of the dignity of all mankind in this movement despite its claim to uphold the family and human life. By attacking the values, dignity, and life-styles of groups they do not like, the Moral Majority leaders deny the existence of moral absolutes, such as human dignity, justice, and freedom, in the name of their very particular (and thus relative) "absolutes." Social class interests dominate this movement. There is no liberation—religious, political, or moral—in it. The movement seems to be merely a tool for extreme right-wing political power seekers.

2

Searching for Certainty

On November 4, 1980, the American electorate spoke with a resounding voice. After several months of concern over widespread religious involvement in the presidential and other election contests, those senators opposed by the National Conservative Political Action Committee were soundly defeated. The presidential candidate supported by this group was elected by an overwhelming majority. The question as to whether such clear intervention in the political process on the part of Fundamentalist Christian groups would be effective or counterproductive received a ringing answer: Yes! The television evangelists and local independent pastors were proved to be effective in the political arena. Without doubt, these conservative voices spoke from a position of power. The most effective way to make conservative religious feeling felt throughout the length and breadth of American society has been discovered. Since so much of the Fundamentalist creed involves an unbroken mythology about the origin and history of America and a stance in values based on faith alone without regard to sociological and psychological studies, it should not be surprising that it is religion, rather than the political-military rhetoric of a Joseph McCarthy or of the John Birch Society that should win the battle.

Appealing to Fear and Uneasiness

Commentators, including religious observers, have long been aware of an increasing sense of unease, fear, and concern in large parts of the American body politic. Earlier, in the seventies, Dean Kelley observed that the conservative churches were growing. He suggested that Fundamentalist-oriented groups were attracting people while the main-line churches were losing them because the more conservative leaders were willing to offer simple, straightforward solutions to problems that the more-informed saw as complex and ambiguous. Conservative churches set strict standards and enforced them. They discouraged discussion or questioning. Rather than finding this confining, many people seemed to think this gave a sense of security. That security in the midst of the insecurity of the 1970s was felt as a positive, comforting thing. It seems plain that in the separatistic theology and the social exclusivism of the independent congregation with its rejection of contemporary moral standards we see a political critique under the guise of church activity. The clearest example of this is the founding of so many independent Christian schools, which goes along with the rejection of the public schools and the rest of society.

It would be easy to say that the reactions of people attracted to conservative religious and political standards were simply shallow or neurotic. It would be easy but unfair to do so. There is much that could upset the average citizen. Indeed, only an unthinking person would not be concerned by the events of the past several decades. To use an overworked phrase, we have been living in an age of uncertainty since the beginning of the cold war in 1947. The eruption of open competition and conflict between the East and West has thrown everyone's life under a shadow. The development of nuclear weapons by competing nations has demolished the myth of American invulnerability. The armed intervention of the United States in several hot-war situations resulted not in clear decisions but in, at best, standoffs as in Korea, or worse, defeat, as at the Bay of Pigs in Cuba, or perhaps worst, a protracted and ultimately losing result as in Vietnam. Suddenly, in the eyes of the average American, the United States was more than vulnerable to nuclear attacks by others; it seemed incapable of defending its position against even small powers. Uncertainty led to a great feeling of insecurity. It is because the right-wing religious commentators are speaking to the real fears and concerns of the public that they oddly include a call for greater armament as part of their religious message. Since the conservatives claim to be biblicists, one would expect them to reflect the Bible's position that it is futile for nations to depend on their own might or on that of allies (Psalms 4:8; 20:7). This clearly shows that the so-called message of the Moral Majority and others is not biblical at all but is a message designed to meet real fears—political fears—among the public.

The age of uncertainty would have been a terrible thing for the citizen to endure even if it had been limited to exterior shocks and military considerations. But in fact, the period of the sixties and seventies has seen rapid, sometimes violent, and alway unsettling social and moral changes within the United States itself. The middle-class, conservative, and conforming citizen has had too much change too fast. Alvin Toffler's description of "future shock" as a disease that affects us when changes come more rapidly than we can absorb them is very apt for our contemporary situation. In such a time of bewildering change a natural reaction is a desire to retreat, withdraw, and to slow down those changes. Such a move backward in the interest of some preservation of the status quo is a textbook definition of conservatism. A list of the concerns highlighted by the Moral Majority illustrates the rapid social changes that have unsettled the less sophisticated elements of the population. These "major issues" include reactions against the enforcement of the separation of church and state on the matter of *school prayer*. Also part of this concern trickles over into *abortion* and *ERA*. These two issues are pushed by the conservative religionists because of their belief that equality for women and readily available abortions violate their view on morality. The same consideration influences their stand on *homosexual* rights. This issue is seen as promoting immorality.

Once those issues are passed, almost all the other major issues of the Moral Majority are clearly political, military, and economic stances taken by those who wish to protect their own financial positions and feel strongly nationalistic. These include *economic policy* considerations which advocate tax cuts and less governmental regulation of business, rejection of *SALT II*, a much *stronger national defense*, an opposition to the *draft* because it might be extended to women, and a strong *support for Israel*. This last item, while in fact a purely military or political issue, is seen as a religious issue by many millennialist Fundamentalists who believe that Israel has a role to play in the events of the last days.

Of the remaining two major issues, *energy policy* is a purely political issue designed to placate businesses, and the *death penalty* is an example of resentment growing out of a widespread belief that criminals—many of whom are minorities—can literally get away with murder. While some Fundamentalists attempt to give the death penalty the cloak of a religious issue, most Christians of all varieties clearly see that the death penalty cannot be considered a Christian mandate.

Ronald Reagan clearly played up to every one of the Moral Majority issues by declaring at the Religious Roundtable meetings in Dallas that lack of old-time religion in public schools had led to increase in crime, drug abuse, child abuse, and human suffering. He told those delegates that government needs to get out of religion but that more religion is needed in government. Reagan expressed doubts about the theory of evolution, saying that creationism ought to be taught in schools. Then speaking to the issue that really drew the television evangelists into the fray, Reagan said the Federal Communications Commission "has shown greater interest in limiting the independence of religious broadcasting than it ever did in limiting the drug propaganda poorly concealed in the lyrics of some recorded songs."

The simplistic, "either-all-good-or-all-bad" logic of the Moral Majority position was demonstrated at the same meeting when, just before Mr. Reagan's appearance, evangelist James Robison preached a sermon which was titled "Either Sound the Charge or Blow Taps for America."[1]

To recap, the position of the religiously conservative coalition that has aided a conservative Republican sweep into power is a reaction to:

the ethnic challenge to white, middle-class dominance;

the same ethnic challenge as it demonstrated the pluralism, actually present in America, which questioned the myth of American homogeneity;

the feminist movement, which has challenged traditional male authority and traditional conceptions of the family (actually, much of the rhetoric about the breakdown of the family is a reaction against the demands and accomplishments of the feminist movement);

the gay movement that challenges the very foundations of masculinity—as well as the traditional idea of the family;

the widespread demand for easier abortions, which challenges the conventional morality supported by conservative churches;

the shift of United States foreign policy from the role of intervention in others' affairs as a leading world power to a more noninterventionist, partnership relationship with other nations;

the loss of prestige of the nation, as in the hostage situation in Iran, growing out of the noninterventionist posture;

the demonstrated vulnerability of the nation, as in the case of the oil embargo and energy crisis which contributed to our humiliation in Iran (it is unbelievable that many people will simply not accept the reality of the energy crisis; even Reagan intimated that there would be no shortage of oil if the oil companies were free to do as they pleased);

the loss of confidence in the dollar and the increasing economic hardship for the lower and middle class brought on by several years of double-digit inflation (this inflation is, of course, directly influenced by the energy crisis as well as by huge government expenditures for defense);

the loss of confidence in national leadership, stemming from the shock of political assassinations in the sixties, the revelation of criminal activity in the White House in the Nixon administration, and the incompetence in many respects of the Carter administration; these considerations of lack of confidence hold equally true for members of the House and Senate, of both parties, a number of whom have been charged, and some convicted, of criminal acts.

Just thinking about the very real changes, challenges, and crises that have characterized American life since 1960 is enough to upset anyone. The fact that phrases like the "age of uncertainty," or "crisis and challenge" have become popular does nothing to change the fact that there are real issues, real problems, and taken as a whole, they are important enough almost to paralyze a sensitive person. There is nothing off base about the conservative concern for America. Equally so, there is nothing wrong with religious people bringing their belief systems to bear upon social problems. After all, what the main-line churches have practiced and preached for decades cannot be wrong just because a conservative does it. Nonetheless, there are some reasons for concern. These reasons involve the relative lack of sophistication of proposed conservative solutions and even the lack of factual accuracy in the conservative reading of the political situation. It is difficult to see how private immorality has great bearing on national security. It is just as difficult to see how government regulation or the lack of it can make any real difference in the finite supply of natural resources like oil. Perhaps even more disturbing are some of the underlying assumptions of those who support the Moral Majority positions. These presuppositions include an obvious confusion of the civil religion of America with Evangelical Christianity. Civil religion has been and will remain a major problem for the church. However, there are assumptions and attitudes that are even more frightening than the identification of the nation with the kingdom of God. These are the often undisguised feelings of resentment, anger, frustration, vengefulness, and narrow-minded declarations of certitude that represent characteristics of those who are attracted to authoritarian and totalitarian movements. The terrible certitude that one knows who the enemy is and the triumphant assertion that one knows the solution are frightening in their implications for America.

The November, 1980, election was a great victory for Mr. Reagan, and the more extreme members of the religious right wing were not backward in claiming the credit for his victory. Paul Weyrich of the Committee for the Survival of a Free Congress spoke out the day after the election, taking credit for the victory and expressing his distaste for Mr. Bush as vice-president. He then aggressively warned Mr. Bush that his political future was in jeopardy if he did not wholeheartedly embrace the conservative cause and also gave the same warning to Mr. Reagan. Success breeds great confidence.

Weyrich issued a naked political threat. Such an attitude makes moderates and liberals feel that their worst fears about the right-wing victory are justified. I should, in all fairness, say that Mr. Falwell and others have not made such threats.

At this point it is important to be clear about the depth of conservative Christian support. Surveys have shown that there may not be the kind of power available to the religious Right that it believes it has. For example, in November of 1980 only 48 percent of the electorate voted. This does not show an all-consuming passion to turn Right on the part of the public at large. Of the 48 percent who voted, only 51 percent voted for Reagan. This means that the Reagan victory rested on the vote of only one-quarter of the possible voters in the United States (26 percent). Considering all the publicity and the many real issues that surrounded the election, it is difficult to see just what specific issues would cause a majority of the electorate to turn out, if they would not in this case.

The very moot question involved is just how much of Mr. Reagan's victory is due to the support of the religious right wing. Clearly, NICPAC and its allies did make a contribution. However, that contribution may not be as large as is claimed. It may well be the case that the Moral Majority made its impact on the senatorial contests simply because it hammered away on vulnerable points in the affected senator's records and philosophies. The Moral Majority thus is a part of the mass of voters who elected Mr. Reagan but does not really make up a majority of his supporters. Surely the support of the Teamsters' Union was very helpful to Mr. Reagan, and this support had little to do with the religious Right. What we are faced with is a situation in which the more extreme members of the religious Right will make claim to a power they may not possess. Mr. Reagan's cabinet appointments after the election do not show much sharing of power with the religious Right. Sorting out the real dimensions of right-wing religious support is a vital and necessary task. Greg Demer in "A Shift Toward the Right? Or a Failure of the Left?" in *Christianity and Crisis* for December 22, 1980, has begun to analyze the data carefully.[2]

Religion's Contributions to Life

Life is fragile. In order for life to exist at all, certain conditions must be met. Even the simplist organisms must have a favorable environment and nourishment. A human being must have air, food, water, and shelter. But when a person has all these things, he or she may not exist above the level of a prisoner in a concentration camp or of the man Friday, rescued from death by Robinson Crusoe. To live truly human lives, people must have other people. And to live with other people means that there must be an order of some kind, a society, and ultimately a center made up of people who direct that order, a political state. The requirements of the citizen of a state may be only those of a consumer and producer. But to live intellectually and emotionally, to live at the level of the fully human, there must be meaning in life. One of the most central elements of human meaning is freedom. Philosophies and political systems exist to find and convey meaning to people and, in many cases, to insure freedom. Throughout our history the major conveyer of meaning to human beings and, therefore, a major source of freedom has been religion.

"Religion" comes from a Latin root word which means "to bind together." Before anything else, religion with its myth and ritual, its teachings and commandments, binds human beings together and gives a sense to their lives. Out of religion grows not only the meaning for individual lives but also the meaning of the social order people inhabit. In helping us to discover who and what we are and identifying the meaning and value of other human beings, religion establishes a human order. Religion is a universal human interest and need. Modern thinkers sometimes forget that. Because the values of the Judeo-Christian tradition have been widely accepted far beyond the boundaries of the church since the Renaissance, becoming part of the teachings of philosophy, literature, history, and political science, some contemporary thinkers have made the mistake of thinking of those values as outmoded and weak. The religious values of the West have never been lost, but they have been "secularized," shared out, becoming the basis of many secular disciplines called the humanities.

Throughout the years of the United States this insight, that religious values are still alive and have somehow become secularized, has come to public attention from time to time in religious criticisms of political issues. At no other time, in any decade of American life, is religion recognized so clearly as it is during elections. Then it becomes clear that the old verities have some currency among the population. The oft-remarked need for public officials and candidates to appear more moral than the average citizen—the problem that so bedeviled Ted Kennedy—rests on just this fact: that the old religious values, in a secularized form, are the common values on which not only American but also all Western societies are based because only these values finally give meaning to human life. This fact is so obvious that it is almost invisible. Travel in a Moslem country, even of the modern sort, makes clear to a non-Moslem how basic the principles of Islam are to that state. Even travel in Communist China, with its many revolutions of culture and attempts at atheism, reveals a society that still finds its meaning in leadership by Confucian-type wise men (like Mao) and its meaning in the balanced harmony of life expressed in the Chinese concept of the Tao.

Religious commentators have long spoken of American civil religion and of the pseudo-religion of Communist and other totalitarian regimes. These insights are valid: many so-called scientific and atheistic social orders are really disguised forms of religion. But the truth lies far deeper. All religions are civil religions. All social orders, because they must be based upon values expressed in ideas that convey meanings important to the people who make up those orders, are, at bottom, religious. Religion binds men and women together. There are many kinds of religion, and there are many kinds of social order. A civil religion in the sense that Martin Marty and other commentators have described it is simply a construct in the abstract of beliefs that long ago were lodged in the body politic and that are raised up as a kind of shadow theology, either by the supporters of such a religion or more generally by church-oriented citizens. The churches and other organized expressions of religion smaller than the totality of the state, often find civil religion offensive. Religious values that have fragmented from organized religion and lodged in the state have at the same time remained in the church where those values may be given a different expression or, more likely, where those values are jealously guarded as the sole property of organized religion.

Because religion gives meaning to life, all religion is authoritative. Religion is, as Paul Tillich remarked, an expression of ultimate concern. In society, the people who pay the most attention to the phenomena of ultimate concern, to establishing content to propositions that express human ultimate concerns, and to the implications of those concerns are known as theologians, philosophers, and ethicists. Men and women deeply attracted to the study of this ultimate concern and who professionally proclaim and teach these propositions have become known as ministers, priests, rabbis, and evangelists. There are no such religious leaders without authority, in the derived sense, for such propositions about ultimate concern claim a universal authority themselves. While human reason or wisdom is generally respected and forms the basis of many ethical directives and the application of many religious values, behind most religious pronouncements lies the claim that the author of religious values is God, the supreme authority. A religion without some sense of its derived authority would not be a religion at all. There are no religions, no matter how tolerant or liberal, that do not claim some degree of authority over human life. This claim may be indirectly and silently made in a secular, pluralistic society, or it may be stridently made; in which case, religious leaders exercise prophetic roles in criticizing the state and their fellow citizens. While they have no monopoly on the claim to authority, we might observe that the more conservative forms of religious organizations have generally laid the most vocal claim to authority, sometimes claiming to speak directly for God, blurring the perception of the derived sense of their authority even in Free Church Protestant forms of expression.

None of this is harmful or wrong in a free society. Indeed, the criticisms and teachings of many religious voices are needed so that one sole interpretation of religious values is not allowed to swamp out all opposition. The constitutional provision that there should be no established religion was not meant to create a religionless society but to preserve the integrity of various faiths and the integrity of the state. In this way there can be not only religious freedom but also secular freedom for all men and women who are allowed to find the interpretation of their ultimate concerns for themselves. Basic values (often called human values because, though originally religious values, they have been so long separated from the established churches) and civil rights (really legal expressions of these basic human values) have become the norm for American society. These values and rights can be challenged or supplemented by opposition from or support of both clearly religious voices and secular voices.

Unlike many other societies which may be equally democratic and nurturing of the human welfare, the United States stands in a unique position of founding its ultimate human "religious" value *in the sanctity and social freedom of the individual human being.* In a pluralistic society, in more than political rhetoric, the individual person as voter and expresser of values in his or her day-to-day life stands as the ultimate authority. The United States remains the first great experiment in the social contract. In such a situation the question of authority, the question as to what values are authoritative, and the question as to how much organized religious values should affect the social outlook, has always been and will always be a problem. The moment the problem is solved, the experiment will be over and the freedom of the individual will only be a chapter in history.

The Religious Right Wing and Politics

The issue involved in the influence of the Fundamentalist right wing of Christianity on the present political situation is precisely this: Is the right wing strong enough *to answer finally* the question as to what is *the* interpretation of our religious values, and therefore will it transform us into a "Christian republic" in which we are free to believe in and act in only one way? No matter how wholesome that way of believing and acting may be, the closure of the conversation between varying interpretations of values and the ending of the experiment in freedom of beliefs and life-styles will be the end of freedom as we understand it in the United States. We will have exchanged the insecurity of freedom of the individual for the security of the determination of our personal values by religious leaders and groups. There will be, at that point, no freedom even for those who sincerely profess the approved interpretation of such values. Like Parmenides, the Greek philosopher who declared there was no empty space between atoms and consequently nothing could really move, such a fixation on one interpretation of values will freeze us into the immobility of bees trapped in amber. We will have no way to move, no way to grow.

It is interesting to note that public conversations of spokesmen like the Reverend Jerry Falwell have become more moderate since the election was decided. Falwell has declared that he and his followers have no desire to establish a Christian republic. He declares that he is for pluralism. Falwell has said on public television that his group is interested in principles, not individuals, and it does not think it is necessary that candidates for public office be born-again Christians. All this sounds very middle-of-the-road and politically aware. The problem is that Falwell often sounds a far different note in his own broadcasts and in his writings.

RELIGIOUS PIED PIPERS

Perhaps the depth of the media blitz from the Fundamentalist Right can be gauged by the fact that Mr. Falwell now begins to sound like a moderate compared to some of the other leaders like Paul M. Weyrich. In the case of the hard-line leaders we see proof of the after-voting poll that revealed only 8 percent of those who voted in the 1980 election were very interested in religion and that most of the persons interested in religion voted for the original "born-again candidate"—Jimmy Carter. What is at issue in a number of the positions insisted on by the religious Right are reactionary fears, feelings, and beliefs that have little or nothing to do with religion. In the demand of people like Weyrich that Vice-President Bush get on the conservative bandwagon and that President Reagan not forget who helped elect him, we see issues that sound strangely similar to the Know-Nothing party of the nineteenth century and the xenophobia that the older American settlers expressed toward Catholic and Jewish newcomers after the middle of the nineteenth century.

A previous generation demonstrated how nativism or America-firstism can become mixed with Christianity and be presented as a political platform. I am thinking, of course, of movements provoked by the Reverend Carl McIntire, who has gained much media exposure by attacking what he calls Communists in the churches; Myers G. Loman, who formed the Circuit Riders in 1951 to fight so-called socialism and communism in the Methodist Church; Edgar C. Bundy, who founded the Church League of America to attack the Federal Council of Churches; and the most famous of all, Billy James Hargis, who began the Christian Anti-Communist Crusade. Of course, people in this earlier radical Christian Right camp, including Hargis and McIntire, are still on the scene. It is at least possible that the present Christian Right has gained insights into organization and party line by studying these earlier crusaders.

It is interesting to examine what Harry and Bonaro Overstreet call the "Radical Rightist line." Writing in *The Strange Tactics of Extremism,* the Overstreets say:

> Those who are now on top—in government, education, church council, labor union, foundation, or whatever—must be pulled down: they are Communists, pro-communists, or dupes.
> Those who are on the outside of the citadels of advantage and

exclusiveness must be kept outside; their efforts to become equals and insiders are Communist-inspired;

Wherever America as a nation has become entangled with outsiders—as in the United Nations and the Alliance for Progress—it must disentangle itself; international bodies are Communist-controlled.

If this reduction of the Radical Rightist line to a set of axioms seems to be a *reductio ad absurdum,* it is nonetheless disturbingly accurate in its essentials.[3]

Paralleling this earlier "Radical Rightist" line, expressed by the right-wing groups of the sixties, we find a strange similarity in that the various Christian Right groups of today *also agree upon a single party line.* The four major organizations—Christian Voice, Moral Majority, Religious Rountable, and the National Christian Action Coalition—work together closely with other conservative groups, such as the Conservative Caucus and the Committee for the Survival of a Free Congress, cooperating on zeroing in on what they call fourteen key moral issues. These include such things as opposition to the drafting of women, calling for increased national defense budgets and also calling for tax cuts, for the death penalty, and for the rejection of the SALT II treaty. *Time* magazine of October 13, 1980, says:

All the groups work closely together: their leaders gather every other Thursday over coffee in Washington to plan strategy with such conservative political groups as the Committee for the Survival of a Free Congress, and the Conservative Caucus. Christian Voice has compiled a list, widely circulated by Moral Majority and Roundtable as well, of how Senators and Congressmen voted in 1979 on 14 key moral issues. It praises votes not only for school prayer but for the Kemp-Roth bill to cut income tax rates 30%; condemns votes favoring not only abortion but the Equal Rights Amendment. The rightists claim to find religious grounds for all these stands. Says [Richard] Zone: "We can talk about a balanced budget as a moral issue. The Bible says you should not live in debt."[4]

It is interesting to note that the unanimity of the right-wing Christian line turns up over and over again. For example, a letter and leaflet sent to me during the days before the November, 1980, election by the Faith America Research and Educational Association of Scottsdale, Arizona, contained some of the same points about the presidential candidates as those listed on a sheet issued by Ohio's Moral Majority, Inc., which was distributed at the local high school and brought home by one of my children a few days before the election. Both sheets deny that they are partisan; but it is interesting that Ronald Reagan is the only one of the candidates that is shown to be "right-thinking" on both of the handouts. Indeed, Anderson and Carter are declared on one or the other or on *both* sheets to promote homosexuality, to be against the support of Christian education, against new tax deductions for church giving, to be for federal control of all church youth camps and conference grounds, and for support for the "religion of secular humanism." The obvious intent is that a religious person who read and believed these sheets would want to vote for Reagan.

The Threat of "Secular Humanism"

The mention of the "religion of secular humanism" gives a clue to both the similarity of the new Christian Right to the old Christian Right of McIntire and Hargis and also to its difference. What has happened is that the old conspiracy theory of McIntire and Hargis that revolved around communism has been replaced by a conspiracy theory that revolves around so-called "secular humanism." Indeed, there is a book, *Secular Humanism: The Most Dangerous Religion in America,* written by Homer Duncan and distributed by Missionary Crusader of Lubbock, Texas. This concept is developed by Tim LaHaye in his book *Battle for the Mind* (Revell, 1980). LaHaye, in an interview printed in the *Wittenberg Door* says:

DOOR: Why do you call your group the Moral Majority?

LAHAYE: We believe we represent the overwhelming majority of the American people. More importantly, we represent the miminum moral desires of the majority of the people.

DOOR: Do you really believe that you represent the minimum moral desires of the majority?

LAHAYE: Look. Gallup says there are 60,000,000 born-again believers. There are another 60,000,000 who are what I call "pro-moralists." (Catholics, Mormons, etc.) Then there are anther 50,000,000 "idealistic moralists." That represents the 84% of the people in this country who still believe the Ten Commandments are valid.

DOOR: What, then, do you think are the crucial moral issues today?

LAHAYE: We think that abortion, homosexuality, pornography, prayer in the schools and family protection from government interference are among the most crucial issues.

DOOR: The obvious question is, of course, if the majority of Americans have minimum moral desires that agree with the ones you represent, then why do we need an organization like yours to "educate" them?

LAHAYE: We have been led to Sodom and Gomorrah by a hardcore group of committed humanists who set out over a hundred years ago to control the masses. They have us in a stronghold. There are only 275,000 of them, but they control everything—the mass media, government, and even the Supreme Court.

DOOR: So the masses have been duped by these 275,000 humanists?

LAHAYE: Yes. Humanists believe in the evolutionary flow of history. They believe that everything is changing so they feel required to change whatever is in existence. They attack the status quo simply because it's the status quo. They have taken the time honored principles that have been good for the family and a moral society and changed them and they've changed them for the worse. They have changed the divorce laws. Abortion has been made legal. Homosexuality was once illegal; now that's been changed. These humanists won't be happy until they've torn down all the laws against incest. Humanists feel they are the elite gods. They feel they need to run the masses because they are too dumb to know what's good for them.[5]

Mr. Falwell cannot escape his connection with this kind of thinking. Immediately before the November, 1980, election I received a so-called "Congressional Petition on Moral Issues." This turned out to be a simplistic form that amounted to a request for a donation. But the letter, signed by Mr. Falwell, sounds much like Billy James Hargis. It says in part:

Is Our Grand Old Flag Going Down the Drain?
Dear Friend:
I have bad news for you:
The answer to the question above is "YES!"

Our grand old flag is going down the drain. Don't kid yourself. You may wake up some morning and discover that Old Glory is no longer waving freely.

Just look at what's happening here in America:

—Homosexual teachers have invaded the classrooms, and the pulpits of our churches.

—Smut peddlers sell their pornographic books—under the protection of the U.S. Constitution!

—And X-rated movies are allowed in almost every community because there is no legal definition of obscenity.

—Meanwhile, right in our own homes the television screen is full of R-rated movies and sex and violence.

—Believe it or not, we are the first civilized nation in history to legalize abortion—in the late months of pregnancy! Murder! How long can all this go on?

I repeat: Our grand old flag is going down the drain.

And not just here in America—we have broken our word with Taiwan because we are afraid of China.

We are giving away the Panama Canal, so we won't "offend" a leftist government!

And besides all that, our President has signed a SALT II treaty with the Russians that will make us a second-rate power in three years . . .

. . . and one day the Russians may pick up the telephone and call Washington, D.C., and dictate the terms of our surrender to them.

And Old Glory is down the drain, forever.

It was mentioned that the present Christian Right has essentially substituted the abstract—and empty—concept of "secular humanism" for the concept of communism of the old Right. The Overstreets made some keen comments about the older Christian rightists that have validity in seeking to understand the present Christian Right.

The Overstreets observe:

> For themselves, these ministers and laymen claim a maximum religious freedom. But like the Communists, they combine their demand for an untrammeled freedom to propagate the truth with a rigidly intolerant will to prevent the propagation of error: which is to say, of any doctrinal, political, or economic view that differs from their own.

It has been said of Stalin that, on the one hand, he revised Leninism to whatever extent his own version of expediency required while, on the other hand, he reduced this same Leninism to so rigid a set of formulated phrasings that he could identify "revisionists" by their slightest verbal deviation from these—and could proceed to liquidate them. These doctrinaire Rightists of whom we are speaking might well, in this particular sense, be called *Stalinist*.

The term would fit them more accurately, in fact, than does the all too carelessly applied term *fundamentalist*. It is true that they call themselves fundamentalists. It is also true that, for complex sociological reasons, the Rightists have been most successful in peddling their brand of anti-Communism in those parts of the country where religious fundamentalism prevails. But we ought not to jump from this fact to the conclusion that religious fundamentalism and Radical Rightism just naturally go tandem.[6]

In criticizing the logic or illogic of the older Christian Right, the Overstreets summarize the shortcomings of this kind of thinking done by the Christian Anti-Communist Crusade but most clearly seen in the John Birch Society party line:

First, then, the Society creates confusion by its loose and irresponsible resort to derogatory labels.

Second, it fosters the belief that a totalitarian form of organization, with directives handed down from the top, is inherently stronger than one that operates by what Welch calls "debating society methods."

Third, it works to persuade people that the only part of the world-wide Communist threat about which they really need to be concerned is that of the internal conspiracy.

Fourth, by labeling as Communist-inspired or Communist-controlled a host of indigenous American efforts to solve pressing social and economic problems, it acts as a brake upon social ingenuity at the very time when we most need to find American ways of coping with colossal forces of change.

Fifth, while it is specific about what it is against, its program for dealing with our twentieth-century complexities is limited to generalized platitudes.

Sixth, it encourages its members to believe that they are acting like responsible American citizens when they echo a leader's stereotyped pronouncements and work hard at tasks set for them by this leader.

And seventh, it advocates dangerously oversimplified solutions to problems beyond our shores—as when it promotes the belief that "it would still take only a few companies of U.S. Marines" to drive "Castro and his Communists out of Cuba, by force if necessary."[7]

The Overstreets hold that, in their zeal to fight communism, the right-wing *actually serves* the international Communist movement.

It does this because it weakens serious thinking about the challenge of communism and vilifies all those who would seriously try to do something about it. Vice versa, the Christian Right today might well do disservice to the cause of religion as well as to the cause of freedom by its misidentification of the problems we face in the modern world. Sometimes it is better to do nothing than to take the wrong medicine.

Without doubt, most of the people who voted for Reagan did so without much regard to the blandishments of the right-wing evangelists. It seems probable that economic issues were more important than religious ones in deciding the election. The very list of issues promoted by Moral Majority and its allies revealed that economic considerations and questions of national prestige and strength were closely related to the campaign mounted in the name of religion. There is a very distinct flavor to the key *moral* issues promoted by the religious Right in 1980: *that is, its antireligious bias*. The religious Right opposed "born-again" evangelical Christians like Jimmy Carter and Senator George McGovern precisely because they stressed love for the poor and the oppressed. Jesus, the prophets, and apostles made such love the recognizable sign of biblical faith. Tim LaHaye makes this negative judgment on helping the poor and hungry clear in his *Wittenberg Door* interview.

DOOR: Surely you believe that world hunger is a much more important moral issue than prayer in schools?
LAHAYE: That is an individual issue. The real question is are you helping people most by giving them bread to eat or by leading them to a vital life changing experience with Jesus Christ and then showing them how to become self-sufficient?[8]

LaHaye defends his position, seemingly denying the Christianity of Mr. Carter, saying, "I shook hands with him twice and got absolutely no spiritual response."[9] His real concern seems to be declared in the kind of slogans reminiscent of the old Right.

The government today is legislating immorality. It is making it easy for people to sin. . . . Either the church is going to become morally active and set moral issues as the dominant standard for its elected officials or we will will be overrun by humanist thought by 1990.[10]

The intent of the religious Right is shown by the "scorecard" for members of Congress put out by the Christian Voter's Victory

Fund. (See Appendix B.) On that scorecard Father Robert Drinan, a Catholic priest, was given a zero. Bob Edgar, a Methodist minister, was given 10 percent. John Buchanan, a Republican and a Baptist minister from Alabama, was given 33 percent. Paul Simon of Illinois was given a 13 percent. And Richard Kelly, who admitted taking $25,000 in the ABSCAM affair, received a 100 percent rating. It was not morality or religious belief but the positions that congressmen took on very conservative and economically selfish voting issues that determined the score given by the Christian Right.

The desire to keep money in the hands of those who now have it by cutting aid to the poor at home and abroad and by strengthening the country so it can have its own way in the world, along with the desire to protect very profitable religious businesses, is the real spirit behind the Christian Right. Perceiving a threat to its private enterprise of public broadcast, schools, and fund-raising drives, the new religious Right has dropped its decades-old refusal to take part in politics on religious grounds to embrace the conspiracy theory of the older religious Right. It is only necessary to create a fictional threat in order to mobilize the unthinking; the selfish, who think very clearly, are quite ready to support this cause. For this reason we have people like Falwell and LaHaye creating another mythical enemy, the secular humanists. As LaHaye says:

> The humanist overlords are determined to stamp out religious rights. The Christian has become the number one enemy. We are in a war but only one side is fighting.
>
> I'm not saying that we should drive the humanists out of the country. This is a free country. Humanists ought to be free to live here, but I don't think they should be our leaders and make our policy because they misrepresent the majority.[11]

Characteristics of the Religious Right

It is never safe to characterize large groups of people. Nevertheless, over the years a number of studies have been made of the kinds of people drawn to extremist or single-issue movements. These are the kinds of persons often attracted to the independent, Fundamentalist churches, the religious cults, and extreme right- and left-wing political parties. Generally, those attracted to the various movements which make up the Moral Majority—which on closer inspection may well be revealed as a minority—are of the lower middle class and are attracted by the certitude claimed by authoritarian and totalitarian movements. They are what Marx called the "lumpen proletariat" or shopkeepers. Such persons are incensed by inflation, higher wages for labor, and the success of the very rich. They are outraged at the prestige given to the professions and unmoved by the humanitarian message of the church. Such people are angry, frustrated, vengeful, and defiant because they are unsure of themselves and confused by the rapidly moving events around them. Such people have worked hard; they feel that some of the power and prestige that society has to offer should be theirs, and yet they feel it is denied them. Rather than "the good Christian middle-class people" getting their reward, they see feminists and homosexuals, minorities and the unemployed receiving consideration by the government. They declare this immoral because they feel left out. Persons such as these greeted Hitler in the thirties and Robert Welch in the sixties and now greet the religious Right in the 1980s. For them there is a conspiracy, whether Communist or humanist. They think there must be a conspiracy against them, for they cannot see that they have already received their reward.

Our present situation of crying for a rebirth of morality is no different from such social upheavals by threatened classes in other places and times, from fifth-century Athens that destroyed Socrates to the Lu of Confucius to the London of Victoria to the New York of Prohibition. What is different is the super-religious tone and color of the contemporary resentment; whether the reaction is political (as in the Moral Majority) or personal in life-style (cults, sects), our rebellion is against things as they are. If Paul were living today, he could say of the United States what he said of the Athenians in Acts 17, ". . . I perceive that . . . you are very religious" (v. 22). If patriotism is the last refuge of the scoundrel, then religion as a mask for human activity is surely the first. If this implies that the Christian Right is not truly religious, that implication is intended.

Whenever the right wing rises to prominence in a society, democratically-minded persons become fearful of the abuse of political authority. This is not a vague fear but a very real concern based on historical experience—the experience of Germany in the Third Reich being firmly in mind. There *is* need for authority in life, authority in both the religious area and in the governmental area; but experience has shown that the connection of these two areas of authority too closely poses real threats for individual liberty. Whether the state rules the church or the church rules the state, the effect is the same. There is too much power lodged in too few hands to allow democracy to exist in such a situation. The framers of the Constitution wisely decreed the separation of church and state and further divided the powers of government into three independent areas: executive, legislative, and judicial. Generally, the electorate has been afraid to lodge too much power in too few hands. The separation of powers has probably declined as a real description of the way things have been in America over the last half century. The great emergencies and needs of the Depression, of World War II, of the cold war, and of the many wars fought since that time have brought great powers to the presidential office. At the same time the raised conciousness of racial, sexual, and ethnic groups in America, aided by the interpretation of federal law by the independent courts, has increased the range of individual liberties. It is not the power of the presidency that has angered the people who make up the Moral Majority but the power of the independent courts to administer justice in an even-handed manner, which the new members of the middle class have taken as a threat to their own power, that has raised the charges of "communism," "humanism," and "immorality." It is interesting that the lame-duck Congress in November, 1980, while still controlled by the Democrats, chastened by the conservative victory, took as its first action the passage of legislation prohibiting school busing to promote racial balance in schools. This was led by one of the heroes of the Christian Right, Senator Strom Thurmond of South Carolina, who once bolted from the Democratic party and formed a segregationist States Rights party and ran for president. It is hard to see Christian morality in blatantly racist legislation. Nevertheless, the so-called Christian groups listed school busing as one of the immoralities they wished to eliminate.

The Christian Right has misused the name "Christian" and the term "conservatism" in politics. It has reduced Christianity to a series of yeses and noes, to simplistic questions, and to a pattern of certain behaviors. It is not unlike the religious cults in this reductionism. Finally, the Christian Right expresses a juvenile desire to have pat, absolute answers to every possible question, an attitude fostered by Fundamentalism and highly developed in cultism, that can only lead to the loss of ability on the part of the persons to think for themselves. In this sense, the radical Christian Right does serve as a possible framework for the rise of totalitarianism in the future. Fundamentalistic sectarians, religious cultists, and right-wing extremists seldom seriously ask themselves, "What really is the situation?" Nor do they ask, "Can I really reduce the problem of our times to a series of questions or issues on which there are only two possible answers?" Theologically, this position is heretical, being gnostic in that it views Christianity as a set of propositions to be believed, a set of questions to be answered; and it is Pelagian in that it puts righteousness in the realm of human works and behavior rather than in confidence in God. Biblical religion teaches us that Judaism and Christianity rest on trust, on confidence, on faith; not on questioning, not on answers, and not on the acceptance of one or more propositions or positions as the right ones. Even the question "What must I do to be saved?" is pre-Evangelical, asked from a pagan perspective. The New Testament tells us that while we were yet sinners, Christ died for us, the Godly for the ungodly. Traditional Evangelical faith holds that we are justified by grace for Christ's sake through faith which is given us as a gift from God. As it is a free gift, it is not an achievement of which we can boast, but a fountain of goodness that we are then directed to share with the lost and the lonely, the hungry and the poor, with the wretched of the earth who, like ourselves, have to do nothing to merit God's love and our love but simply to be. When the Christian Right takes the Bible seriously, then mainstream Christians will be able to take it seriously. Until then we must oppose it as a deception designed to gain material benefits for those who wrongly claim to be moral.

3

The "Born-Again" Movement

In 1972 Dean M. Kelley, director for civil and religious liberty of the National Council of Churches, created quite a stir when he published *Why Conservative Churches Are Growing.* Kelley addressed the growing discussion since the late 1960s that concerns the statistical decline in membership and contributions to the middle-of-the-road, main-line Protestant denominations. The great liberal calls to engage in social action in the 1960s, joined later to a widespread church participation in the arguments about the Vietnam War, had ended in a dissaffection from the mainstream churches by conservative, rural Protestants and increasingly conservative small-town and urban Protestants. The result was some unhealthy budget figures and loss of church membership for the United Church of Christ, the United Presbyterian Church in the U.S.A., and several other groups, including the United Methodist Church, the Presbyterian Church in the United States, the American Baptist Churches in the U.S.A., and the Episcopal Church. Polls also (as in the Gallup report of May 25, 1968) purported to show that there were an increasing number of people saying that religion was losing its influence on the people. None of the mainstream church leaders denied some loss of membership and funds. The question was, "Is religion still alive and healthy and taking on a new form?"

Kelley believed that he had uncovered evidence that conservative churches were growing. There was an increasing awareness of independent Fundamentalist congregations attracting disaffected people from other groups, Kelley zeroed in on some religious groups that were definitely growing at rates far beyond an expected average. Unfortunately, Kelley was wrong in his appraisal of the appeal of very conservative church groups. What Kelley did was to mingle together classic cults and the more conservative Christian churches to come up with his thesis that strong religions, that is, churches which demanded belief in a strict set of doctrines and values and high conformity to life-styles unlike those prevailing in society, were experiencing growth while mainstream churches were declining.

It is not hard to show Kelley's error. Among the groups he counts as "conservative churches" are the church of Jesus Christ of Latter Day Saints (the Mormons) and Jehovah's Witnesses. Few *orthodox Christian conservative* believers would accept Mormons or Jehovah's Witnesses as Christians and even less as conservative Christians. What is more, Kelley's thesis, which has been used to publicize the strength of essentially Baptist Fundamentalist groups, gave as the third of its fast-growing conservative churches the Lutheran Church—Missouri Synod, which is hardly a Free Church Protestant group in the general American tradition. What is more devastating to Kelley's thesis was that the Missouri Synod fell apart in church strife between genuine moderates and the few ultraconservatives who had seized power in the Synod only a few years after Kelley's book appeared.

Dean Kelley's book, of course, is but one prominent example of a general religious tenor that characterized the 1970s. So much did the Free Church conservative wing of Protestantism capture the thinking of the decade that magazines from *Time* to *Newsweek* and beyond claimed that the title of the 1970s should be the "Decade of the Evangelicals."

We have become so used to media figures telling us there are sixty million Evangelicals in America that we forget the simple logical step of asking, "What is the basis of those figures?" This magic figure of sixty million came from another Gallup poll that reported that sixty million people claimed to have had a "born-again" or life-changing religious experience. This figure was taken up by the conservatives as if it reflected sixty million people in their churches. It does not mean that. Actually, many millions of these respondents are members of mainstream Protestant churches or the Roman

Catholic Church. And many millions more are believers who report strong faith and life-changing experiences but belong to no church at all. The huge numbers of Evangelicals reported by the press tend to disappear when they are examined carefully.

I believe that playing fast and loose with figures does a disservice to the genuinely Christian conservative groups that have matured greatly over the last few decades and have experienced a much smaller rate of growth—but a real growth—in the same period. No one is served by falsehood. Nor is the Christian cause served when commentators offer us techniques to build churches or to conserve membership by pandering to human weaknesses. Unfortunately, Kelley also makes that mistake. He tells us that strong religions grow and weak ones decline. The characteristics of strong groups that he lists are indicative of the kinds of congregations he sees as viable. I believe, however, that even on conservative theological grounds these characteristics must be considered sub-Christian.

According to Kelley, among the traits of a strong religion are:

1. *Commitment*
   —willingness to sacrifice status, possessions, safety, life itself, for the cause or the company of the faithful
   —a total response to a total demand
   —group solidarity
   —total identification of individual's goals with group's[1]

I think a fair reading of this characteristic would say it perfectly describes the People's Temple at Jonestown. Not only that, the idea of submerging the individual into the group is the basic principle of facism as it was discussed by Mussolini in his writings and preached by Hitler in his speeches. Kelley says,

The appreciation of individual worth and freedom is one of the highest achievements of modern man, but it does not do much for social strength. If each member is unwilling to give unquestioning obedience (or even much questioning obedience) to a leader or group, it makes for an atomistic aggregation of individualists rather than a cohesive, deployable organization.[2]

What Kelley does not say—and what those religious rightists today who call for a conforming life-style don't say—is that freedom is the exact opposite of this characteristic of total commitment. The scholar who studies beliefs like this must clearly identify them as authoritarian, to be precise, as fascism.

2. *Discipline*
—willingness to obey the commands of (charismatic) leadership without question
—willingness to suffer sanctions for infraction rather than leave the group[3]

Kelley tells us that this means willingness to expose our deepest feelings and convictions to public scrutiny. It means giving up our deepest ideas when leaders tell us we should believe something different or act in a way we would not otherwise act.

3. *Missionary Zeal*
—eagerness to tell the "good news" of one's experience of salvation to others
—refusal to be silenced (Acts 5:26)
—internal communications stylized and highly symbolic: a cryptic language
—winsomeness[4]

There is, of course, nothing wrong with this trait on its face value. We could all wish that all Christians were more missionary oriented than they are. This is an area in which the mainstream churches can and should learn from the smaller, conservative Protestant bodies. However, the matter of stylized internal communications presents a problem. Charismatics, for example, who are always saying "Praise the Lord," seem to put off people as much as they attract them. We know that each of the religious cults has its own highly stylized and cryptic language. This may be a necessary psychological trait, but I think it has its drawbacks. Above all, we should remember that not only genuinely pious people are missionary minded. Communists, socialists, fascists, even aggressive atheists show the very same characteristics of extending their messages. In Christianity the content of the message is always more important than the technique used to spread it.

4. *Absolutism*
—belief that "we have the Truth and all others are in error"
—closed system of meaning and value which explains everything
—uncritical and unreflective attachment to a single set of values[5]

This absolutistic tenet is one of the most unlovely characteristics of extreme Fundamentalism, of Marxism, and other forms of totalitarian thought. There is no doubt about the psychological strength that grows out of such a position. But there are very real issues involved concerning the Christian character of such a position. Absolutism leads to intolerance, and intolerance is a lack of love. In the case of extremely right-wing religious groups, part of the Moral Majority, this absolutism leads to movements to stop the teaching of evolution in public schools, prevent sex education, and in general pervert the free exercise of the mind on the part of citizens that are not part of the absolutistic groups. This conception of knowing everything also lies behind the growing so-called Christian school movement and promises to be a real threat to all public education in the United States over the next few years. Whatever the claims we may make to the absolute truth of Christianity, and we may make those claims in a responsible manner, no thinking Christian should or would make authoritarian, absolutistic claims that would violate the freedom of persons who don't share our Christian convictions.

5. *Conformity*
   —intolerance of deviance or dissent
   —shunning of outcasts (*Meidung*)
   —shared stigmata of belonging (Quaker garb and plain talk)
   —group confessions or criticisms (Oneida)
   —separatism[6]

Of course, there can be little objection to a freely elected life-style within a group. The human race would be the poorer without the enrichment of the special life-styles of groups like the Quakers, the Mennonites, and the Amish. Nonetheless, history reveals that there is such a thing as being *too* religious. The *meidung,* or ban, certainly can be used in unchristian ways, as was demonstrated in recent years by the Pennsylvania man who offended the bishop of his church and was placed under a ban that broke up his marriage, took his family away, and destroyed his business. We are reminded of the punishments inflicted upon members of the People's Temple by Jim Jones. Conformity purchased at the price of love and human dignity cannot be considered by Christians.

6. *Fanaticism*—Kelley speaks of this trait as "all talk, no listen." He speaks of living in a cloister, of keeping oneself "unspotted from the world."[7] This is in contrast to the reserve that characterizes weak groups, and we must admit that reserve has characterized

many members of mainstream churches. This is a reluctance to talk about one's faith and certainly a lack of desire to force one's beliefs on others. Reserve is not a proper Christian characteristic, to be sure, but considering the well-documented cons of evangelism carried out by religious cults and the unthinking nature of fanaticism per se, one must seriously ask if the cure is not worse than the disease. The fanaticism that conservative Christians decry in cults they certainly should not celebrate when practiced by themselves. Once more I have no doubt that such fanaticism is a strong characteristic that makes for a strong group. The efficacy of this trait and some of the other traits are probably not to be questioned. But what is to be questioned is whether or not a group that would be characterized by these six marks would be Christian. Christianity, by virtue of its belief in a God of truth, love, and justice, must give up a claim on every tactic that does not fit in with its beliefs about God. There are some things we cannot do and still claim to be Christian. Some of these traits very clearly fit that characteristic of being unchristian.

Evangelicals and the Right Wing

The concept of Evangelicalism or the "born-again" movement (more recently called "Neo-Evangelicalism") is almost a sacred concept today. Nevertheless, some careful analysis of the movement and its ideology is needed. We should test the thesis that conservative religion is the wave of the future.

First of all, Evangelicalism is not a monolithic movement. Anyone who is respectful toward Evangelicalism will immediately recognize that not all Evangelicals are politically conservative in the sense that Moral Majority and Christian Voice represent themselves as being. To the contrary, many Evangelicals, specifically those who have come to call themselves Neo-Evangelicals, are socially active and progressive in their thinking. Evangelicals for Social Action, headed by Ronald Sider (an outstanding Evangelical thinker now teaching at Eastern Baptist Seminary near Philadelphia) stands in roughly the same social position as the mainstream Protestant churches did during the 1960s. These Evangelicals side with conservatives on family issues and also decry abortion. But they criticize other conservative groups, saying, "If human life is sacred then surely this means something about the nuclear arms race, too. In Scripture, the social question mentioned most often is the plight of the poor." The editor of *Sojourners* magazine, Jim Wallis, quoted in a *Time* magazine article, agreed, "In the activities of the Christian right, all that remains of Jesus is his name." But Christian Voice's Richard Zone was quoted as saying, "It's time for godly folk to have an input into government."[8]

Anyone with a grasp of theology realizes that the only way one can posit a massive Evangelical presence in the United States is to ride roughshod over very deep theological dissensions. First, there is a deep division between Calvinists and Arminians, not to mention a severe split between Fundamentalists who deny the validity of speaking in tongues and the charismatic movement. Then there are the divisions between Protestants and the Roman Catholic charismatics who are indiscriminantly lumped in with the Evangelical movement. It takes great sleight of hand to see all these divergent tendencies as part of one movement. This is to overlook the more modern and realistic divisions between the ultrasectarianism of independent congregations and the older, more commonly accepted Evangelical groups like the churchly Reformed and Christian Reformed churches, the various Methodist groups with their connectionalism, and—the concluding bombshell—the fact that the term "Evangelical" is originally and officially the title of the Lutheran churches, most of whose members probably would not fit into the contemporary "Evangelical" category.

Nevertheless, there is a recognizable Evangelical movement in the country today, whether we call it a new or an old movement. There is a conservative tendency in much of the theology and this has affected, in ways both good and bad, the life of the average congregation. But the Evangelical, or Neo-Evangelical, movement is not the real force behind the Moral Majority movement. Nothing said here is directed toward theologians or church leaders in the present revival of conservative biblical beliefs. But the so-called born-again movement or the Evangelicalism that purports to be behind the conservative side in politics is other than and different from the Evangelicalism of Fuller Theological Seminary, the Christian Reformed Church, the Church of God (Anderson, Indiana) or any other institution or denomination long recognized as a responsible conservative voice within the larger universal church. The "born-again" movement that impinges upon politics is a media event, a phenomenon of the electronic church created by radio, television, and computer-operated mailing lists and is at best *para-church* in its structure and not sect or denomination oriented, or theologically orthodox at all. As was mentioned earlier, the "electronic church" is Docetic, without belief in the need for organization and grass-roots work.

To summarize: The "born-again" movement, or Moral Majority, is not conservative but radically *reactionary*; not Evangelical but *sectarian* to the point of theological heresy; not orthodox but *heterodox;* is not attached to the traditional groups and institutions that are correctly known as conservative or Evangelical in any of the recognized theological traditions, nor can it be considered an actual majority. Like so many other images created by the mass media and Madison Avenue publicity techniques, its power lies in its control of communications and constant repetition of simplistic slogans. It is a papacy without a church behind it, a product created of paper and electronics, and above all, it is not a church or a wholesome voice for the biblical message. Its greatest threat, religiously speaking, is its power to defame true Evangelicals and to strip their congregations of members, or more likely, of their members' financial support. One Southern Baptist pastor told me that a family in his church had said they had cut down their pledge because they were sending their money to one of the television evangelists. Later that family called him in the middle of the night and asked him to come over to help settle a family dispute. He said he was very tempted to tell them to call long distance and ask the television evangelist to make a house call. In short, the true Evangelicals, perhaps more surely than the mainstream clergy, will find the popular Evangelicalism of the electronic preachers parasites on church life, not contributors to it.

But the greatest danger of the "born-again" movement is its political effect. We must be fair and say that it would be hard to prove that the Moral Majority style politicking made a great contribution to the Republican victory in 1980. But it did contribute. Of course, there is nothing wrong with the Republican Party taking political power. Christianity cannot be partisan, no matter what the personal preferences of the Christian. But what is significant is the terribly conservative tone of the various Republican victories. More to the point of the influence of the "born-again" movement is the more demonstrable strength it played in defeating one half dozen senators who were considered enemies because of their stand on social issues, although many of them were traditional Evangelicals of the highest moral standing.

Again, it is a free country, and there is nothing wrong with religiously oriented groups participating in a free, democratic process. But just here we need to be wary. The genuine Evangelicals in their national magazine, *Christianity Today,* presented very responsible editorials and articles on the elections that did not become cultic in their support for one side or blind to every issue but the simplistic list supported by the Moral Majority. A very fine editorial, "Getting God's Kingdom into Politics," was presented that was genuinely evangelical but was quite unlike the position of Falwell and his followers. While in support of the vigorous stands those religious lobbies took for morality and social change, the writers went on to say: "Unanimity among Christians is hard to find, either in politics or theology." Then the magazine mentioned favorably the position of Evangelicals for Social Action (ESA). The editorial went on to criticize Moral Majority and Christian Voice for not emphasizing the ESA stand of a special concern for the poor, for peacemaking, and for stewardship of the earth's resources. The editorial continued:

> In fact, probably more space in the Bible is devoted to calls for justice and the care of the poor than to the fact that human life is sacred, though none can deny that both are biblical mandates. The concerns of the religious lobbies will appeal to a broader range of Christians to the extent that they emphasize these other equally biblical principles of justice, peace, stewardship of our resources, and care for the poor, as well as profamily and prolife issues. It is a case of "these ye ought to do but not to leave the others undone." Too narrow a front in battling for a moral crusade, or for a truly biblical involvement in politics, could be disastrous. It could lead to the election of a moron who holds the right view on abortion.

The rest of the editorial is so sound that I reproduce it here. The difference of a genuinely evangelical perspective from that of the born-again Moral Majority leaders is clear-cut and profound:

> *Are all evangelicals necessarily politically conservative?* No. Ask Mark Hatfield that question. Or Jimmy Carter. Or John Anderson. Or anyone who reads *Sojourners, The Other Side,* the *Wittenberg Door,* the *Church Herald,* or the *Christian Leader.* "All evangelicals" agree on very few things, but at least they agree on the most important

things; in one God who in Christ chose to invade our planet in order to redeem men from sin and its consequences; the substitutionary death of Jesus Christ on the cross as the means by which God himself completely settled the score of man's sin; his own sovereign role as the Supreme Judge of all the universe; the need for a personal relationship with God through faith in Christ; and the call of every Christian to discipleship and a life of sacrificial love in service to God and our fellow men. Everything else is application and secondary—even politics. . . .

But there are differences in viewpoints. We insist that it is possible for an evangelical who believes in the inerrant authority of Scripture to be a political moderate, or even a liberal.

Is there only one "Christian" position to take on each of today's complex issues? No.

We get the impression that some evangelical lobbies on the political right, as well as liberal lobbies on the left, want us to believe that theirs is the only truly Christian position on all issues. How can a policy board of evangelical Christians, without access to vast amounts of intricate political data, emerge from a meeting and announce that it has arrived at *the* Christian or moral position on lifting sanctions against Zimbabwe, for example? Or how can its opposite number, a body of liberal theologians, demand the reverse as *the* Christian position? . . . .

The Bible isn't always explicitly clear on how its principles are to be understood and applied to every specific issue. These applications are not always divinely given in the Word of God. Our best efforts to be biblical and moral on current political, social, and economic issues are still limited, very fallible human applications of the infallible Scripture. We must be prepared to recognize, therefore, that sincere and conscientious Christians may apply these principles in different and sometimes opposite ways. Recognizing the diversity in the body of Christ, Christians must allow for these differences in application of God's truth.[9]

The fact that *this* brand of Evangelical thinking about moral issues is far removed from the single-issue politics of the Moral Majority ought to be clear to everyone. Contrast the responsibility of *Christianity Today* to the National Affairs Briefing in Dallas whose leaders told a cheering crowd of 15,000 that they were for:

- Constitutional amendments to permit voluntary prayer in schools and prohibit abortion.
- Death of the Equal Rights Amendment.
- Stiffer penalties for pornography and drug dealing.
- Limits on federal intervention in schools.
- A fattened defense budget.[10]

Bill Keller of the *Congressional Quarterly* has observed:

Even architects of the movement concede that, as political forces go, theirs is a blunt instrument. Sometimes they use strong-arm tactics. For example, Mr. [Robert, of Moral Majority] Billings says that when Rep. Mickey Edwards (R., Okla.), a staunch conservative, initially balked at signing the petition [for prayer in schools], a Roundtable lobbyist persuaded an Oklahoma television preacher to castigate the congressman on the air.

Mr. Edwards signed the petition, but Mr. Billings says the episode left conservative Christians with a reputation for heavy-handedness that may hurt them next time they need a favor. "In our enthusiasm," he says, "we sometimes do or say things that we wouldn't do if we were a little more experienced and mature."

Some backlash has developed among religious leaders and lawmakers who are offended by the idea that "Christian" equals "conservative."

"It's all playing on people's dark side," Tom Getman, an aid to Sen. Mark Hatfield (R., Ore.), an evangelical with a liberal voting record, says, "They say nothing about social justice. Nothing about the nuclear arms race. Nothing about our militarism or materialism."

"Generally, it is a good movement," Bailey Smith, president of the 13-million-member Southern Baptist Convention, says. "I think we have to really be careful, though, in identifying all conservative political views with Christianity. . . . The way some of these men talk I think they're more excited about missiles than about the Messiah."[11]

It's interesting to note that Mr. Billings underscored the thesis of this book that the so-called Moral Majority is largely a matter of unenlightened zeal. It wouldn't do the things it does if it was true to genuinely Evangelical standards. Writing in *The Christian Century* for October 8, 1980, Robert Zwier and Richard Smith criticize "Christians Politics and the New Right," saying that the new fundamentalist Christian political groups claim "they have the correct, biblical answer and that those who disagree with them are not fit to hold public office because of their immorality."[12]

Zwier and Smith go on to observe:

Despite the validity of their recognition of a Christian political responsibility, their call for repentance, and their generally nonpartisan appeals, we have several serious disagreements with these groups. The first has to do with their explicit link with ideological conservatism and the implicit suggestion that this ideology is more attuned than is liberalism to the principles found in the Bible. The idea that the principles of God's revelation can be neatly subsumed under the rubric of a humanly devised ideology is pretentious. Any full examination of biblical standards will disclose a subtle blend of "conservatism" and "liberalism." The Bible is full of passages mandating a concern for the poor—a focus too often lacking in laissez-faire conservative circles. The Bible does not see government as the satanic evil which the conservatives decry; rather, the government is a divinely ordained instrument.

The point here is not that liberalism is closer to the Bible than conservatism but that we are using the wrong level of analysis when we seek to portray either ideology as more Christian. God's will is not subordinate to ideological predispositions; it supersedes them.

Futhermore, there is evidence that these new groups take an inconsistent view of the role of government. For the most part, they desire to limit its power. Yet on certain issues they call for more government involvement. For example, they seek a broad role for government in eliminating abortion, in restricting the rights of homosexuals, in taxing for new weapons systems whose need is unclear, and in mandating prayer and Bible reading in public schools. In short, they do not want government intervention when their own freedoms are at stake, but they are willing to use the power of the government to force life-style changes on others. One does not have to be a proponent of abortion or homosexuality to see the inconsistency. If it is not right to use the government to force one group to tolerate the life-style of others, then it is equally wrong to use the government to compel the second group to tolerate the life-style of the first.[13]

The church historian Abdel Ross Wentz once remarked that history is made up of a swing of the pendulum of ideas followed by a corrective swing in the opposite direction. At the time I heard Dr. Wentz's lecture, I dismissed his observation (shared by Keith Scott Latourette and other historians) as overly simplistic. Now, in the 1980s, I'm not so sure. It does seem that the permissive and progressive sixties followed the safe and conservative fifties—and then the reactionary seventies followed the sixties. If there is something besides coincidence here, then we'd better hold on to our hats in the eighties! Already we see the self-doubts and self-criticisms of people during the Vietnam era giving way to an "America First" mentality, especially on the religiously conservative Right.

It is possible to understand the whole mass-media promoted phenomenon of the "born-again" movement as a drive for conformity as opposed to the widely variegated life-styles currently existing in America. Certainly one does not have to be a psychoanalyst to deduce from the preaching and writing of the televison evangelists that they feel threatened by many modern life-styles, particularly those of the feminists and homosexuals. Jerry Falwell's book *Listen, America!* demonstrates that he is threatened also by the concept of children's rights. Falwell says:

> Any enumeration of children's rights must begin with the right to life from the moment of conception. We reject public policies or judicial decisions that embody the children's-liberation philosophy: that children have rights separate from those of their family and/or parents. Advocacy of children's rights that does not begin with advocacy of the right of the child to be born is reflective of moral and intellectual bankruptcy.[14]

Recently a young feminist, active in the election campaigns in Ohio, said that she was told that the Moral Majority was opposed to the establishment of shelters for battered wives because they would give government sanction to the breaking up of marriages. This was confirmed by a reading of the proposed "Family Protection Act" introduced by Moral Majority politicians as S.1808 in the 96th Congress, on September 24, 1979. (See Appendix A.) Obviously, the rights of husbands are being chosen for support by law in contrast to the rights of battered wives, and the rights of parents are being chosen over the rights of children who may be battered by their parents.

Falwell goes on to discuss government programs and policies:

> We endorse Senator Paul Laxalt's Family Protection Act and the family-protecting approaches embodied in it, an approach that encourages family, community, and local initiative to support families. We recognize that solutions to family problems will not be found in a proliferation of government programs. We reject the unfounded assumption that bureaucrats or "human services personnel" know better than parents what is best for their families.
>
> The purpose of the Family Protection Act is to counteract disruptive federal intervention into family life in the United States and to encourage restoration of family unity, parental authority, and a climate of traditional morality. The Family Protection Act, S./1808, was introduced in the United States Senate on September 24, 1979. There are thirty-eight separate concepts in the Family Protection Act dealing with such things as education, taxation, welfare, domestic relations, and the guarantees provided by the First Amendment. Everything in that bill supports traditional values, encourages families to stay together, upholds parental authority, and reinforces traditional husband-and-wife relationships.[15]

Falwell's book is a repetition of the clichés of the Christian Right of the 1960s. The sense of a threat to the middle-class life-style and a paranoid fear of communism brings him to recommend cutting off the rights of people leading life-styles different from his own and to advocate warlikeness toward the Soviet Union. At this point we are reminded of what Richard Hoffstadter called "the paranoid style in American politics." Writing in 1964, Hoffstadter was reflecting on the nation's experience with McCarthyism in the 1950s and the Goldwater campaign of 1964. James M. Wall, writing in an editorial, "The New Right Comes of Age" in the October 22, 1980, issue of *The Christian Century,* says, "It is the paranoid Right that is currently making such an impact on American political life." We must remember that the paranoid style of politics can be found on the extreme Left as well as on the extreme Right, but today we are manifestly not much influenced by the extreme Left. By "paranoia" both Hoffstadter and Wall mean that people who share this vision see the world as a place where there are forces aligned against one's nation, culture, and way of life; and they must be stopped before they undermine one's very existence.

In earlier days this paranoid style showed itself in the Know-Nothing and other nativist movements that were prejudiced because of their convictions that groups like the Masons or Catholics or the newly-arrived eastern European immigrants were conspiring to change the way Americans lived. Today we can see that same paranoid style in the Religious Right's sense of threat from liberals, gays, feminists, and the decades-old presence of communism in the world.

Wall says:

It is at this important juncture in American history, when a sizable number of people are uneasy and resentful of changes they do not like and do not understand, that this group of television-preacher fundamentalists has arrived on the scene. Displaying none of the clumsy crudeness of their radio predecessors ("Coming to you from Del Rio, Texas"), these preachers are using media with consummate skill. By seizing upon the resistance to life-style changes that have taken place in this country over the past two decades, they have built an enormously successful religious and political network. The paranoid style has found followers who, in varying degrees, resent what they perceive as the disintegration of religious values. And what is even more significant for the political process, they believe that the federal government has played a major role in this disintegration. We cannot judge the sincerity of this movement's leaders. If they are in the tradition of the paranoid style of previous religious-political leaders, however, their pain over such matters as abortion, homosexuality and pornography may be less authentic than their recognition that they have found an issue to exploit. But there is genuine pain among those who respond to them, in whatever degree, from the casual viewer to the active participant in their conferences.[16]

Martin E. Marty, in the July 15, 1980, issue of *Context* (reprinted in the *Wittenberg Door*), has given us some points to consider about the new Christian right wing. As usual, Marty is insightful and very much to the point. He tells us not to underestimate or overestimate this new group. He reminds us that the huge figures given for "Evangelicals" include many people who will never vote.

Above all, Marty urges us to "understand their hurts and resentments":

> . . .Resentments? They have felt left out in everyone else's liberation. . . Women's, black, Chicano, gay, and other liberation movements leave them behind. The textbooks have been changed to accommodate the sensibilities of Jews, homosexuals, women, and the like. The only ethnic stereotypes one can still use and misuse are WASP, redneck, or backwoods and, to a lesser degree, Catholic ethnic. As one such WASP once told me, "In all their exoduses and liberation plots, I'm Pharaoh." The left-out people not only want in, but they want to run the show. We will make no progress on this issue until the larger public sees the new Christian right as a tribe that feels slighted.[17]

Marty correctly predicted that the "new target will be humanism." He parallels the choosing of this scapegoat with the famous threat of secularism that was trotted out in every pulpit in the 1950s. He says:

> In the 1950's even moderate church people made a bogey out of secularism as the all-purpose scapegoat. Today the Christian right wing is itself so secular in its general mode of existence that it needs a new foe. Watch as the months pass. More and more the leaders will focus on the words "humanism" or "humanist" when they set out on white chargers. That is too bad because there is a noble tradition called Christian humanism. Those of us in the humanities will suffer because we who teach the subjects are called humanists for different purposes.[18]

Marty goes on to urge us not to grant the Fundamentalists in politics the claim that theirs is the biblical program.

There are a few lines in the Bible critical of homosexuals. There are a few lines that the rightists can use to support their opposition to pornography or obscenity and their calls for restriction of freedom on that front. There are no lines they can use for their position on gun control, the Panama Canal, and the like. It takes a special reading of the Bible to use it against the Equal Rights Amendment. The Bible says many things about human life, but the case against abortion is not an unambiguous one. So much for their causes. Now look at the yards and meters of Biblical print spent on calls for justice and mercy and righteousness. Give the new-right leaders all they want for ten years and you will not hear these brought up. Concern for equal justice and for the rights of the poor dominates many a prophetic writing and never shows up here. Now that this new force has entered politics frontally, it merits this challenge: If you want a Biblical program, include more of the Bible.[19]

Marty's insights make a good summary of this study of the electronic "born-again" movement as a disguise for authoritarianism. What we see in the Moral Majority movement is a rise to great influence of middle-class, Midwestern, Southern, Far Western, middle-aged white males who are right of center on every controversial issue from racial intergration to women's rights to homosexuality to drug use to the cold war. As Castro discovered in Cuba years ago, great power comes to a spokesman who says publicly what people secretly want to hear. Falwell and others in the religious Right have had the bad grace to say, with a straight face on television, what most people say with a smirk to their friends. As one of my quite conservative theological students recently observed, "The Moral Majority is actually an immoral minority." Christians are really the minority who struggle against the immoralities of the society in which they live. The Moral Majority actually generates the immoralities of class and wealth and selfishness that the minority of Christians proclaims to be wrong.

4

A Biblical Critique of the Moral Majority

*These are grumblers, malcontents, following
their own passions, loud-mouthed boasters, flattering
people to gain advantage. (Jude 16)*

The platform put forward by the Moral Majority and its
conservative religious and secular allies makes the strong claim
not only to be based on the Bible but also to be the essential message
of the Bible expressed without any qualification. The Moral
Majority therefore invites—although it may not wish it—a biblical
criticism on its claims.

In investigating the pronouncements and writings of the religious
Right, it becomes obvious that there are six important characteristics of its theological position that underlie the demand for moral
reform. All six of these positions tend to be based on one
fundamental theological principle: the identification of the United
States of America with the chosen people, biblical Israel, in the
same fashion as the civil religion criticized by many historians.[1] This
point-for-point identification of America and Americans with Israel
and the children of God is an absolute confusion based on a lack of
perspective that sees the kingdom of God in our national variety of
the kingdom of the world. In all events, the six elements are:

1. Identification of the United States of America with the biblical
Israel.

2. Identification of a part of the population with Christian

righteousness and a moral life-style, resulting in a class and ideological critique of other classes and life-styles.

3. A punitive rather than compassionate outlook on sinners.

4. A militaristic emphasis stemming from the identification of the United States with the chosen people of God.

5. Tactics of intimidation, hate, duplicity, and manipulation.

6. A triumphalism of spirit rather than a call to humble service.

A Mistaken Identification

The identification of the United States with the chosen people is hardly a theological novelty of the Moral Majority. Many groups and movements before them have made the same identification. In fact, the identification of the nation-state with God's favorites is a part of world history, being seen in the British Empire, in German expansionism, and in many other places and times.

Looked at biblically, such an identification of that which *is* with that which *ought to be* is a gross confusion and error. Indeed, it is not too much to say that Old Testament theology itself often points out, in the words of the prophets, that the chosen people cannot be identified completely with even the ancient people of Israel itself. To be a Jew is to be a Jew inwardly and spiritually. To be a part of God's chosen people is to be part of the community of faith and obedience. The act of being chosen by God is not an arbitrary act of favoritism but a choice or election on the part of the Creator for a purpose—the larger purpose of being a light to all other nations and peoples. It is an election to service and to suffering rather than to rule and honor. Every one of the writing prophets could be quoted to underscore this vital distinction. It is not the nation itself, nor is it the people themselves by virtue of their talents or righteousness, but it is God's election in order to show forth divine mercy and power that lies behind the Exodus and the giving of the Promised Land.

> "You only have I known
> of all the families of the earth;
> therefore I will punish you
> for all your iniquities."
> —Amos 3:2

· In the New Testament the identification of God's chosen people with a single nation is seriously criticized and undermined. It becomes clear in the teachings of John the Baptist, the teachings of Jesus and of Paul and the other apostles that the true Israel of God is identified by faith and obedience. It is not identified by race or nationality or whether one is Jew or Gentile—or in the modern parlance, whether one is American or Russian or Italian or Vietnamese or black or white or male or female. The varieties of humanity that can be part of the kingdom of God—the New Testament rendition of the chosen people concept—are endless. Membership is a matter of faith, not of birth or residence.

The Moral Minority

The identification of a part of the population with Christian righteousness and a moral life-style, and a consequent criticism of everyone else, seems at best an exercise in self-righteousness and at worst sheer vanity. More than this, there is an element of deception—perhaps self-deception—in the exclusive identification of righteousness with the members of the Moral Majority. It becomes clear upon analysis of the platform of the Moral Majority and its right-wing allies that the thundering of the righteousness of their group is an ill-disguised class and ideological critique of all other classes and life-styles in America as well as throughout the world. The Moral Majority standard of righteousness is certainly nationalistic, is demonstrably ethnocentric, and from its attacks upon women's rights is clearly male-chauvinistic. None of these positions would be readily accepted by most Christians as the only Christian position.

It is possible to interpret the deep and angry criticism of the welfare system by religious Right leaders as a very thinly disguised form of racism. While this may not be the case—and the Fundamentalist Right has moved away from racism quite a bit—nevertheless it is probably factual to say that the portion of the population that is most outspoken about people on welfare has in mind blacks and, very likely, unwed mothers—and often times it sees these two groups as one. Surely no form of racism can be reasonably called Christian or even religious.

What is more to the point, no criticism of the poor, no addressing of their situation without compassion, can be considered biblical. One does not have to follow Jurgen Moltmann or any other liberation theology thinker to recognize that both the Old and the

New Testaments have a tilt toward the poor. The prophetic literature, full of the renunciation of sin, the background for the criticisms leveled by the Moral Majority, is stout in its defense of the poor. The prophet Amos clearly attacks the well-to-do in many places:

> They hate him who reproves in the gate,
>   and they abhor him who speaks the truth.
> Therefore because you trample upon the poor
>   and take from him exactions of wheat,
> you have built houses of hewn stone,
>   but you shall not dwell in them;
> you have planted pleasant vineyards,
>   but you shall not drink their wine.
> For I know how many are your transgressions,
>   and how great are your sins—
> you who afflict the righteous, who take a
>   bribe,
>   and turn aside the needy in the gate.
> —Amos 5:10-12

Amos goes on to describe the kind of religion God accepts as vital and real, in words that Jew and Christian can never forget:

> "I hate, I despise your feasts,
>   and I take no delight in your solemn
>   assemblies.
> Even though you offer me your burnt
>   offerings and cereal offerings,
>   I will not accept them,
> and the peace offerings of your
>   fatted beasts
>   I will not look upon.
> Take away from me the noise of
>   your songs;
>   to the melody of your harps I will
>   not listen.
> But let justice roll down like waters,
>   and righteousness like an ever-
>   flowing stream."
> —Amos 5:21-24

Along with the male-domination, nationalistic, and ethnocentric elements of the Moral Majority platform, this economic class consciousness reveals a very secular and sinful repudiation of the inclusiveness of the gospel and of the universality of biblical law and grace. Paul shows us the genuine tradition in his ringing description of the Christian life-style:

> For as many of you as were baptized into Christ have put on Christ. There is neither Jew nor Greek, there is neither slave nor free, there is neither male nor female; for you are all one in Christ Jesus. And if you are Christ's, then you are Abraham's offspring, heirs according to promise (Galatians 3:27-29).

Punishment Rather than Compassion

The Moral Majority and other right-wing religious groups definitely show a punitive rather than a compassionate outlook on sinners. The call for capital punishment, severe denunciation of homosexuals, and the insensitive attack upon women who have abortions, do not show a properly biblical grief over sin, regret for the punishment sin often brings as its fruit, or any concern for the persons of the sinners. This is an area the Christian must criticize since, in the simplistic thinking of the Moral Majority leaders, any attack on this point is seen as a defense of sin. But it is our moral duty to call the Moral Majority to task for misusing God's law as a weapon of destructiveness instead of the rehabilitation of the sinner. Love must make distinctions. Genuine law must be constructive. We cannot, even though capital punishment is clearly allowed in the New Testament by Paul, go on to make capital punishment a Christian necessity in society. Surely there is room for many different opinions on capital punishment by equally sincere Christians. The rulers of our age, whom Paul says we must obey, no longer carry a sword but are backed up by a police force with automatic weapons and armed forces with nuclear weapons, and they dispense justice according to laws that are different in many respects from the laws of the Roman Empire. Even so, the present situation may require punishments suitable to the crimes committed and the types of people who commit crimes. Surely no reasonable Christian would argue that the death penalty should be inflicted for the wide range of crimes that were so punished by the Roman Empire. The history of the West shows a growing sensitivity to human beings and their failures as well as an awareness in many lands, including our own, of the relative ineffectiveness of capital punishment as a deterrent to crime. As recently as the eighteenth century, hundreds of crimes in Great Britain were punishable by hanging. Among those crimes was the picking of pockets. Amazingly, pickpockets attended hangings in droves, for the crowds made profitable victims. There is no clear evidence that the death penalty deters crime, and certainly no evidence that capital punishment expresses the highest Christian moral vision as an adequate response to crime.

Even closer to the religious tradition and a good example of the absurdity of claiming super-Christian morality for capital punishment and other harsh responses to antisocial conduct, is to raise the question as to whether the Moral Majority type would like to see the death penalty enforced for the scores of crimes punished by death in the Old Testament. The covenant code in Exodus, chapters 21 through 23, recommends death for persons who strike their parents and even death for those who curse their parents (Exodus 21:15, 17). While we don't approve of parental abuse, I suspect most people would find this penalty absurd—on Christian grounds. We might also mention that the same covenant code prescribes death for a witch, for someone who commits bestiality, and for idolatry. While none of these are activities that we would want to commend, again our Christian conscience sensitizes us to the crimes against love represented by these laws. Just how far does the Moral Majority want the death penalty to go?

By the same token, the attack by the Moral Majority on homosexuals must be tested by the sensitivity of Christian conscience and our feelings that we must love the sinner regardless of the sin. We need make no defense of the morality of homosexuality to suggest that law and punishment have never been effective in eliminating this life-style and that such attitudes toward homosexuals only brutalize the rest of us while increasing the problems of the homosexuals.

In looking at the Moral Majority attack on ERA, women's rights, and feminism, I think even a middle-aged ex-marine like me, who was raised in a male-chauvinistic era, must flatly say that the right-wing position is sheer nonsense. On what grounds are women to be denied equal rights under the civil law? While the male-dominant expressions of Paul are certainly in the New Testament, and the Old Testament shows a patriarchal family structure, are we to be bound to these accidents of history forever? Against the Paul who wrote 1 Corinthians 11:2-16, holding that the head of the woman is the husband, we must oppose the Paul who wrote Galatians 3:28, who said that in Christ there is neither male nor female. In all events, the religious tradition is beside the point here. ERA and women's rights have to do with civil law, the kingdom of the world, and not the kingdom of God or the church. This is another example of the basic confusion of the sphere of the church with the realm of the state. In brief, there is nothing sinful about ERA and women's rights. It would be possible to hold the very conservative religious view about women in the church on scriptural grounds and, in one's capacity as a citizen, support ERA. This is a position seldom seen on the Right because of a confusion of law and gospel and of the two kingdoms or orders that govern the world.

Many sermons and discussions by the religious Right, by Falwell, the 700 Club, and others hold that these groups are not opposed to women's rights but are opposed to the implications of the ERA. Specifically, these implications are identified by the possibility that ERA would legitimatize homosexual marriages and require that women be subject to a military draft, and within the military, be required to serve in combat. Let's examine these critiques.

On the matter of homosexual marriage, only a lawyer could determine that this implication is present in the ERA amendment. Since I am not a lawyer, I will not debate that determination. But let us argue the worst case. Is there any governmental jurisdiction in the world today which permits homosexual marriage? Is such a result necessarily tied to legitimatizing women's rights? I think not. And if the implication is contained in ERA, surely it could be ruled out by an amendment to the law by the legislative bodies or by judicial decisions. It seems to me that this is a scare tactic raised by people of male-chauvinist mentality to attempt to block women's rights effectively. I certainly do not support homosexual marriage, and I do support ERA. I suspect this is true of millions of others. Biblically speaking, the whole charge seems to be a sinful effort to reject the equality of men and women—which Paul declares is the case—in Christ.

As to ERA making women subject to the draft and to combat service, we must observe that the 1980 draft registration law only applied to males. While the Supreme Court is now considering whether or not such a draft registration should include females (and we have no ruling yet, as this is being written), it would be simple to restructure laws on women's rights either exempting them from the military draft or else permitting them to be drafted but exempting them from combat. Lest extreme feminists think I am against full equality, let me say I am not. To be exempted from the draft in no way needs to be a diminishment of women's equality under the law. We do not deny full legal rights to males who are conscientious objectors and who refuse the draft. By the same token, by law, clergymen and theological students are exempted from the draft and suffer no loss of legal rights. Indeed, the majority of the male population is exempted from the draft—or has been up until now, although they may have had to register—on the basis of physical, mental, or emotional disabilities. Men excused from the draft suffer no loss of rights. In the same way, women could be exempted from the draft, as are conscientious objectors, ministers, and the disabled. Why? Because a free society chooses to preserve its values by calling upon some classes of full citizens in a manner different from that required of other classes of citizens. Even in a modern, total war, everyone doesn't fight.

Militarism

Concern with the draft and things military is not limited to the role of women in the Moral Majority mind-set. There is a strong militaristic emphasis by the religious Right, chiefly consisting of calls for more military spending, an increase in the size of our armed forces compared to those of the Soviet Union, and an often-expressed anxiety over the decline of the United States from military world dominance. This is a rather strange plank in a "Christian" platform. The emphasis upon United States military might reveals the nationalistic, ethnocentric bias, and even chauvinistic patriotism, of many elements in Middle America. But religiously this militaristic emphasis is due again to a simple identification of the United States with God's chosen people. Radical rightists' rhetoric, secular and religious, is full of simplistic thinking that casts other nations, particularly the Communists, in a "bad boy" role and sees America as always good. While we need not defend the merits of the American way of life and we can confidently say that communism has caused many more problems than it has solved and does present itself in oppressive and militaristic fashion, this by no means is a proof of the righteousness of every American policy. We are a nation like the other nations and can claim little or no moral superiority over other peoples. We are sinners capable of doing good, often with high ideals, who make many mistakes. In the realm of the world, in the state, the best that we can hope for is justice; we should not look for moral perfection. Moreover, we should not attribute moral perfection to any government or nation. " 'None is righteous, no, not one' " (Romans 3:10). Ironically, many of the religious rightists interpret the Revelation to John in a sectarian manner, seeing present-day history in terms of the visions of the seer. They might be well advised also to take something of the cynical attitude of John toward the state. He could say "that whore of Babylon" and speak of the "mark of the beast" about the government of his time. John was certainly in no danger of confusing the state with the church or, worse, with the kingdom of God.

None of this is to be taken to mean that we cannot be patriotic and be Christian at the same time. We can. But we can never be super-patriotic or chauvinistic. Love for our native soil and fellow citizens, no matter how deep, is not an excuse for acting unjustly toward other peoples. We can affirm our right of defense of our liberties without legitimatizing efforts to take advantage of other countries. Genuine love always includes the desire for justice.

The rather belligerent language of the religious Right makes obvious the gap between its vision of morality and that of the New Testament. Throughout the teachings of Jesus and Paul there are warnings that we must restrain the use of force, curb punitive instincts, and practice forgiveness to the point of turning the other cheek and even clearer statements that we ought not to resist evil by force (Matthew 5:38-48). While the mainstream of Christianity has never embraced pacifism, no fair reader of the New Testament can deny the pacifistic implications of Jesus' teachings. There is certainly no militarism in the Gospels. We are to love our enemies and pray for those who persecute us. We are not to resist evil. We are told that the peacemakers are blessed and that the merciful shall have mercy. It is the poor in spirit and the meek who will see the kingdom of God and inherit the earth (Matthew 5:1-11). While the church may not be pacifistic, it certainly can never be militaristic as long as its foundations are in the Gospels. The kingdom that is coming is one of peace. And as Jesus made clear in John 18:36: "My kingship is not of this world; if my kingship were of this world, my servants would fight, that I might not be handed over to the Jews; but my kingship is not from the world." Paul states in Romans 14:17: "For the kingdom of God is . . . righteousness and peace and joy in the Holy Spirit." He continues only a few phrases later, "Let us then pursue what makes for peace and for mutual upbuilding" (Romans 14:19). Paul lists peace as one of the fruits of the Spirit in Galatians 5:22.

The clear teaching of Scripture is away from Christian involvement with military force and to the cultivation of every element in a person's common life that makes for peace. As Paul states in 1 Timothy 2:1-4:

> First of all, then, I urge that supplications, prayers, intercessions, and thanksgivings be made for all men, for kings and all who are in high positions, that we may lead a quiet and peaceable life, godly and respectful in every way. This is good, and it is acceptable in the sight of God our Savior, who desires all men to be saved and to come to the knowledge of the truth.

Questionable Tactics

The aggressive note seen in the Moral Majority's inclination toward punitiveness with regard to life-styles other than its own and militarism with regard to other nations is connected surely to a certain meanness of spirit that becomes open and obvious in the tactics of intimidation, hate, duplicity, and manipulation that religious right-wing speakers used many times during the course of the 1980 election. Senator George McGovern has labeled these attitudes and actions as "moral intimidation." He quotes Senator Barry Goldwater, surely a respectable conservative, as saying, "If they disagree with you one bit, you're a no-good s.o.b." [2]

McGovern goes on to point out that punishment, revenge, targeting, and other such hostile words are the political vocabulary of the religious rightists. This usage is based on a self-righteousness and a smugness that know no bounds. They are absolutely sure they are the chosen ones, and consequently anyone who disagrees in the slightest with them is evil and is not to be given consideration. For this reason political opponents are not just to be opposed and outvoted but are seen as enemies to be eliminated. Targeting seems a favorite word to these people. McGovern says,

New Right activists are best understood not as political operators of the kind familiar to both Republican and Democratic parties but as political theologians, priestly exorcists, in the service of a cause without content.[3]

There is nothing in the Judeo-Christian tradition to legitimatize these aggressive tactics. Measured by the standards of the Sermon on the Mount and by Jesus' words that we should love our enemies, the unchristian and immoral nature of such Moral Majority tactics is plain. There is a definite violation of Paul's injunction that we should speak the truth in love (Ephesians 4:15). There is also a turning away from the fruit of the Spirit, as mentioned in Galatians 5:22-23: "But the fruit of the Spirit is love, joy, peace, patience, kindness, goodness, faithfulness, gentleness, self-control. . . ." Paul speaks plainly against these kinds of tactics just two verses later: "If we live by the Spirit, let us also walk by the Spirit. Let us have no self-conceit, no provoking of one another, no envy of one another" (Galatians 5:25-26). Continuing his theme in the next chapter, Paul advises these groups—and all of us: "Brethren, if a man is overtaken in any trespass, you who are spiritual should restore him in a spirit of gentleness. Look to yourself, lest you too be tempted" (Galatians 6:1).

In every human enterprise, and most certainly in politics, sin creeps in. If the religious Right had merely made some moral blunders or become hostile and intimidating in a few instances, we could overlook this, since the Moral Majority leaders are merely human and not sinless. But the occasional lapse is not the case. The considered, systematic and unrelenting bombardment of the religious Right is intimidating, hateful, manipulative of the public's fears and baser emotions. Morally speaking, the Moral Majority is immoral, both by the standards of the secular world and by any interpretation of biblical principles.

Triumphalism

The religious Right shows the theological stance historically known as *triumphalism*. Triumphalists claim to be elevated over all other forms of belief and life-style rather than issue a call to humble service in attempting to heal the many problems of our society. The triumphalist note has generally been associated with a heavy emphasis on personal evangelism as well as on a reactionary criticism of whatever life-styles are prevailing·in society. Considering the background of the electronic preachers who coordinate the Moral Majority program, we ought not be surprised at this superior attitude taken toward other religions—note the comment, made by a fundamentalist Baptist leader, that God doesn't hear Jews' prayers—as well as toward those whom the triumphalist Christians feel are secular or immoral. "If you're not like me, you're just nothing" seems to sum up this attitude. Such a self-centered, in-group, and generally ethnocentric position laid the foundation for the Crusades and fueled anti-Semitism throughout Western history. Measured by the humility of Christ and his inclusiveness of the poor, the sinful, tax collectors, and lepers, this triumphalism is shown up as the self-righteousness of a particular group of human beings rather than as obedience to the gospel. It was the Lord, after all, who said, ". . . he that is not against you is for you" (Luke 9:50).

Many Christians, before the Moral Majority came along, made the same mistake of taking the proclamation of the gospel as a sign that they should proclaim triumph over all other peoples and movements. They missed the gentleness and love, the service and forgiveness, the healing and the helping that characterize a geniunely Christian moral attitude toward people and society. We are to act out of compassion, love and concern—not out of a sense of superiority—when we deal with others. We are to take the lower seats and not to proclaim ourselves the majority. Self-righteousness is never a Christian response to sinfulness. We often forget that the parable of the prodigal son is also the parable of the elder brother and that the elder brother's sin was self-righteousness. The Moral Majority would do well to study Luke 14:7-14 and 15:11-32. I am afraid that there are a lot of elder brothers making speeches who forget that Christ told us not to invite our friends, brothers, kinsmen, or rich neighbors when we give a dinner, but rather to invite the poor, the maimed, the blind, and the lame just because they cannot repay us. Jesus promises a blessing at the resurrection of the just for those who live by this love. What kind of love is it if we salute only those who salute us in return? There is no room for triumphalism, for intimidation, and for aggressive attacks on other people's beliefs or lack of beliefs in a truly Christian moral stance.

Finally, the Moral Majority might well consider the Letter of Jude, where we are warned against ". . . grumblers, malcontents, following their own passions, loud-mouthed boasters, flattering people to gain advantage" (v. 16). We should not listen to such people but rather seek to "save some, by snatching them out of the fire; on some have mercy with fear, hating even the garment spotted by the flesh" (v. 23).

5

Prescription: A Healthy Faith

In many ways the recent turn of ultra-conservative religious people toward politics is a healthy move that ought to be encouraged. It is not the involvement of church people in politics that presents us with a problem, but it is the perennial failure of so many of the Fundamentalistic mind-set to see reality clearly. It is the content—nationalistic, militaristic, and economically selfish—of the Moral Majority platform that gives America its problems today, not the involvement of religious people and beliefs in such issues. I am tempted to say in a paraphrase of Scripture, "All those things you should have done, but you should have taken the opposite side." We must remember that quietism, an ideological separation of religion and political life, is the usual attitude of Fundamentalism. The current grasping after political influence by mass media Fundamentalist evangelists is very different from the approach of Fundamentalism in the first seventy years of its existence. Staying away from politics is no more religiously healthy than is the use of class disaffection and the fueling of fear of communism as the television evangelists currently do. Healthy religion must be something more than absolutist domination or *laissez-faire* indifference.

We can understand the appeal of anyone who claims to have the answers in the uncertain situations we have faced as citizens over the past several decades. The problems of war and peace and justice and declining natural resources and of governmental corruption—all the historical elements picked by apocalypticism to announce the flaming end of the world—when properly understood, can provide a fertile setting for the proclamation of the gospel.

I believe people are uncertain; they are looking for spiritual security. I have noticed this in the small parish I have supplied for ten years. We have experienced a burst of new growth—people who say they are frightened and confused by Iran and Afghanistan, the threat of renewed hostilities with the Soviets, inflation, and the breakdown of traditional moral standards and social roles. We have the opportunity to witness to these people in a genuine, Christian way. We had best do so; for if we do not, the sectarian revivalists will certainly incorporate them—or worse—the cults will attract them. Because we are an emotional people, the Fundamentalist-sectarian strategy is highly effective.

Our task is to proclaim a religious faith that is healthy in the spiritual and psychological meanings of that term. We must escape the shallow thinking that religion per se is a good thing. Religion can be healthy or unhealthy. Unhealthy religion is theologically speaking, idolatry. It may be the idolatry of something outside the self, such as the nation, one's race, or one's class. It may be the worship of the self. The Moral Majority and its allies make much of the so-called religion of secular humanism. Recently the secular humanists (and there are not very many of them) brought out a new magazine, *Free Inquiry* (winter, 1980-1981). The humanists made it very clear that it was the rise of Fundamentalism in politics that caused them to found their new magazine. Clearly these humanist leaders who declare, "Secular humanism places trust in human intelligence rather than divine guidance. . ." are idolators in the biblical sense. They worship man instead of God. But many of the extreme conservatives of the Moral Majority are as idolatrous as the secular humanists. Indeed, their idolatry seems to be of a grosser order than the humanists.' The humanists are all elitist intellectuals and are typical gnostics who worship the powers of the human mind. These secularists come from all nations and races and are biased only toward nonintellectuals and not toward races or classes. Unfortunately, the Moral Majority type tends to have an idolatry of a particular kind of human being, the kind of person he or she is or would like to be. The divinity such a person mistakenly ascribes to white, middle-class males is not fully extended to women and children and is emphatically denied for homosexuals, Communists, and "non-Evangelicals." In place of this mistaken rendition of the gospel we must proclaim a healthy faith.

The elements of a healthy faith must embrace gospel as well as law, grace as well as demand, and, above all, must be based upon feelings of compassion and solidarity with others, not on selfishness and rejection. There is no good reason to be against sin if we are not *for* the sinner. We have no right to condemn if we do not at the same time hold out the promise of pardon. As theologians from John to Paul to Augustine to Luther to Calvin to Barth to Brunner to Moltmann have declared, the center of the Christian proclamation is the cross of Christ. The cross stands both as the revelation of sin and the revelation of God's grace which has opened the way for the overcoming of sin in all who have faith. To be truly a "moral majority" or, better, to be a loving minority, Christians must not harp upon life-styles that trouble them but lift high the cross that overcomes all troubles. We must simply confess Christ, whether we are liberal or conservative, Fundamentalist or modernist. If we do not do that, we are simply not Christian, no matter what label we claim for ourselves.

I propose that healthy religion should be genuinely evangelical, based upon the counsel of Scripture and the experience of the church with the Holy Spirit throughout two millennia. This view of Evangelicalism, the vision of Luther, is something other than the content given the term by popular movements today. It simply means to confess Christ and to function in society as, in Luther's words, "little Christs" to our neighbors. To confess Christ in this manner is to point to the cross as gracious invitation and free forgiveness, not as a talisman or shibboleth which one must accept or reject. To point to the cross is not to announce a gospel of success or to give points to those who have "made it" in the world. This triumphalism of wealth is actually the gospel of self-fulfillment based on positivism, which grows out of atheism and materialism. To be true Evangelicals, we will not stroke ourselves and others like us with positive strokes that tell us we are naturally good while declaring that everyone else is a sinner, a rebel against God's law.

A healthy Evangelical faith will differ from most of the religious as well as psychological ideas of today, for the cross tells us something about humanity as well as about God. We will confess that we cannot save ourselves, nor can we cooperate with God in remaking ourselves. Pelagianism has been condemned over and over again as a heresy. It is only the cross, the objective deed of God in Christ, that is the means of our salvation. The ethic of the Bible, a response to the grace of the covenant God, differs widely from the teleological (purpose-oriented) ethic of the new Right which wants morals that will build up the family and the nation.

As Luther says in the *Large Catechism* (Creed, Article I): "If we believed this article, it would humble us, it would terrify us. Daily we sin with eyes and ears, with hands, with body and soul, money and property, all that we have; particularly do they sin who oppose the Word of God."

Revelation, as Luther, Barth, Calvin, Tillich, and others tell us, always reveals something about ourselves as well as about God. We believe the cross, and all of God's Word, reveal that we are sinners, rebellious, selfish, and egocentric.

And the cross reveals something about God. "While we were still weak, at the right time Christ died for the ungodly" (Romans 5:6)—without any merit on our part, before we were even born, God did something to change our situation—God sent his own Son to be the propitiation for our sins. God does the saving.

My thesis is that the main-line churches do proclaim genuinely Evangelical theology, but we do not live in a culture attuned to true Evangelical theology. We do confess Christ as the ground and agent of our salvation, but we confess him in a religious environment that uses the term "Evangelical" and the term "salvation" often in unbiblical ways.

Religion in America, in the popular sense, is a human-centered, subjective, emotional, nonsacramental (or nonordinance), Book-oriented affair. The operative words are experience, decision, belief. And we are moved to these beliefs, decisions, and experiences *emotionally* by preaching that declares over and over, "the Bible says," appealing to the fear that the world is degenerating, moving toward some absolutely ghastly Second Coming. So confessing Christ becomes tantamount to saying, "Stop the world. I want to change it to suit myself."

We are then invited into a little company of the pure and urged to separate ourselves from the apostates around us. We form up around an infallible Book that tells us of the horrible things that are coming and of the great secret: We pure ones will escape into another dimension (that's apocalypticism—based on dispensation-alism). Whether we like to think so or not, when we evangelize the public, that's the kind of scenario we set off in the nonchurch member's mind; for we are all conditioned by the mass revivalists of radio and television.

It is a simple step from the mass apocalyptic, Fundamentalistic revivalism of popular religion to out-and-out cultism, like the People's Temple, the Children of God, the Way International (all of these are Protestant church heresies), or the more exotic but basically similar Hare Krishna (Iscon), Unification Church (Moonies), Divine Light Mission, and Scientology cults.

When you abandon the centrality of God's divine initiative—our unmerited election in Christ and the faith given us by God through the proclaiming, loving activity of the one, holy, apostolic, and catholic church—you are on the naked plains of the human spirit where any demon that comes along can consume you.

The Lure of Religious Authoritarianism

We have observed that religion helps us discover who we are, gives us a sense of identity as persons and as members of society, and tells us something of the deepest values of life. Religion gives us this sense of life, that the universe is rational and that there is a mind behind it that is directing even the problems and turmoils of history toward a certain end. In short, religion helps provide authority in life. In ancient civilizations, religion ultimately was the authority behind the state. The emperor was either the son of God or consecrated by the gods. From the Pharaohs to King David, the figure of the divine stood behind the throne with a sword. Even Paul recognized that behind the throne of heathen rulers there were principalities and powers, angelic or divine forces that demanded respect in ways that go beyond the respect for physical force or the legitimacy of public acceptance. The Roman Caesars claimed to rule in the name of the gods, and after Constantine the Christian emperors were, in effect, representatives of the biblical God. During the Middle Ages the political idea of the divine right of kings developed. The king of France was put on his throne by the help of Joan of Arc, who had revelations from God. The authority of the Lord and the authority of the state have long been mingled together in Western history.

Even in modern times Western European nations have enjoyed a close connection of church and state. The established church idea essentially makes priests and ministers employees of the state. We need to point out to right-wing Christians that it was precisely to separate the state from the church that we devised the system of government we have in the United States.

Richard Quebedeaux, in *The Worldly Evangelicals,* summarizes the position of Evangelicals in politics in the recent past, saying:

> By and large, twentieth century white evangelicals have either been outwardly apolitical or have taken the conservative position on almost every social, economic, and political issue. For a long time there has been a visible alliance between the evangelical right and center and the Republican Party, culminating perhaps in the Billy Graham-Richard Nixon friendship and the evangelist's public endorsement of Nixon's presidential candidacy in 1972.[1]

Of course, Quebedeaux was talking about Evangelical politics to the end of the Nixon administration. The revelations of the corruption in an administration to which Billy Graham was close surely sharpened the sense of a crisis of authority in America in the minds of Evangelicals. The fact that those who beat the drum loudest for the supposed moral verities (Richard Nixon, John Mitchell) turned out to be amoral manipulators apparently did nothing to shake the confidence of the Evangelicals in the content of the old-time morality. This is surely a case of spiritual blindness; amazingly, the truth did nothing to taint the name of the Republican Party in their view. Indeed, the new Right seems to contain many people who were previously Democratic. The message of the conservatives still is a lure to those seeking authority and stability in life. The often-demonstrated worldliness of those leaders most willing to use moral issues to gather support seems not to have come to the attention of the Moral Majority leaders and their followers.

Sidney Mead noted that conservative Protestantism has long had a weakness for viewing the society around it as something sacred. He says:

> . . . at the time Protestantism in America achieved its greatest dominance of the culture (1850-1900) it had also achieved an almost complete ideological and emotional identification with the burgeoning bourgeois society and its free enterprise system, so that in 1876 Protestantism presented a massive, almost unbroken front in its defense of the status quo.[2]

John A. Lapp of Goshen College in Indiana, in "The Evangelical Factor in American Politics," points out that the conservative, Protestant view of society is not any different from the American-way-of-life mentality of liberal groups. Any criticisms made of Evangelicals can be made of Protestantism in general. Lapp declares, "What is different is that evangelicals who felt alienated from the majority both politically and religiously since the denominational divisions of the 1920s now are again in the mainstream of American life. As many have remarked, these evangelical churches are growing and their views are having an effect on American elections."[3] Lapp sees the reason for this in the exhaustion of the liberal establishment as well as the sense of purpose and confidence the evangelical spirit gives people in a confusing time. This evangelical thrust is also very much a part of the backlash against the reforming zeal of the 1970s. It is, in effect, a search for and a declaration that one has found a source of authority and an authoritative way of life in a time when all values seem to be crumbling. Nonetheless, Lapp, a prominent Mennonite, points up four ways that he sees the evangelical political stance as being off base.

First, the much-quoted desire to restore a nobler Christian politic reflects a serious misreading of history. The past was really no better than the recent past that is being rejected. The idea that America was once a totally Christian nation is trite. It is not a myth; it is a fairy tale. I have discussed this myth of America in my book *The Recovery of America*.[4]

Second, the use of moral and religious language in the political area tends to make the political order sacred. This is the opposite of the biblical outlook. The state has its own reason for being under God—as Luther said, it is the kingdom of the world and is not to be confused with the kingdom of God.

Third, Evangelicals in politics tend toward a confrontationist style. Here the authoritarian nature of right-wing Christianity is clearly seen. Political campaigns and international problems are seen in rigid polarities of right and wrong. America is always seen in the right, and there are calls to organize the forces of right for opposition to communism and domestic evil. This is the aspect of the Christian right wing, both old and new, that is most like the Nazi message of the 1930s and is the most frightening.

Fourth is the most basic flaw in the Evangelical political stance, which underlies each of the three failures listed above. The gospel has been distorted and misused by the Christian Right in an individualistic and privatistic manner. This misunderstanding is possible because of the right-wing misunderstanding of the church. The pessimism of Evangelical eschatology also depreciates the usefulness of social reform and political change.[5]

One does not have to make a great deal of the difficult decades America has recently passed through to establish the point that the past quarter century has been an unsettling time for many. The anxiety of inflation, changing moral values, the relative power of the United States in the world, and apocalyptic revelations of America's dependence upon foreign oil and declining natural resources have tended to make most people feel less secure than they did some years ago. There was a real search for authority in the election of Richard Nixon, but he proved to be a broken reed. The born-again Jimmy Carter was evidently sensed as too weak and ineffective to restore confidence and authority, although both he and Gerald Ford did much to restore confidence in decency in governmental leaders. While Mr. Reagan projects an aura of authority and also of decency, one is tempted to say that the Moral Majority would much rather have a strong leader than a decent one. It is authority people are looking for, and not sermonizing. Mr. Carter surely gave us enough of the latter. We must remember that there was residual strong support for Nixon among conservatives right up to the moment of his resignation and even beyond. It seems that it is the business of a leader to lead—a political belief that may not be wrong in its essentials.

There are at least four psychological elements involved in the attraction of an authoritarian political order that seem to be mingled in the Moral Majority campaign. Some of these are quite worthy motives while others reveal the darker side of human nature. Essentially, I see these psychological factors as, *first,* the search for a strong leader—a father figure, and for a sense of belonging to a viable group—a sense of family (perhaps Mr. Reagan's age was not a detriment but an asset in the election). *Second,* another factor is a search for security and protection in an increasingly dangerous world. We have mentioned the revival of the conspiracy theories of the older Christian Right and the new Christian Right. These theories hold that there is danger both within the country as well as without. Many people want a guarantee of protection from all enemies, foreign and domestic, with the emphasis placed on the domestic ones.

Third, here the shift moves away from the normal and positive to factors that might become dangerous if manipulated by the unscrupulous. The sense of identity given to one by virtue of belonging to an in-group, the Moral Majority or patriotic Americans, is greatly desired. This desire to be part of a group is also perfectly natural, but it has the unfortunate effect of setting up "out-groups" in order to define the in-group. The out-groups of the Moral Majority—Communists, liberals, feminists, homosexuals, those wanting abortions and those leading sexually free life-styles, as well as those on welfare or food stamps—are many. Unfortunately, most racial minority groups tend to become mingled in the out-groups, as do intellectuals and religionists like Jews, liberals, and mainstream Christians, both Protestants and Catholics, who do not share the vision of the Moral Majority. So numerous are these out-groups that it is clearly ridiculous for the Moral Majority to call itself a majority.

Fourth, this defining of the in-group with the correct ideas and behaviors very dangerously gives support to many prejudices: class, sexual, racial, and religious. Immediate moves to retard integration by cutting off funds for busing, and a call by the Heritage Foundation to revive the Un-American Activities Committees of the House and Senate show that the ideological intolerance characteristic of the old Christian Right is very much alive in the ranks of those who supported the Reagan victory in 1980.[6] Black Americans in particular are watching carefully the programs and policies that will be implemented by the new administration.

Searching for a Healthier Religious Faith

When we use a word like "health" or "healthy" to apply to religious faith, it should be obvious that we cannot claim that such a quality of faith can be achieved by education or information alone. If we were to speak of ignorant faith—a word that might fairly be used for some features of right-wing religion—then the answer, indeed the only possible response to such religious ignorance, would be education. But the new religious Right is not the result of

95

ignorance so much as it is the result of negative attitudes, attitudes of hostility and feelings of isolation that have been manipulated by religious leaders for their own purposes, and in recent elections have been manipulated by far Right political leaders who saw in the great mass of religious conservatism the votes they needed to come to power in America. Clearly the church and all people of goodwill can only respond by attempting to promote a healthier, more positive set of attitudes toward God, self, others, and country than are presently being trumpeted by the religious Right.

Let me repeat, feelings are not necessarily changed by the reception of new information; and feelings, attitudes, desires, and hopes fuel human action. Nevertheless, the organized church has the obligation to attempt to make the religious-political situation of today clear to the great mass of the population as part of the task of developing more positive, healthier attitudes. We do not need a substitution of vague, warm, liberal religious ideas for the cold and vengeful ideas promoted by the new Right. What we need are realistic ideas that see the world with its dangers and problems for what it is and go on to stress the possibility of faith and hope and loving concern for all conditions of people.

Part of making the present religious-political situation clear is becoming aware of the background of the electronic religion of the new Right. Johnny Greene, in his article "The Astonishing Wrongs of the New Moral Right," points out that the Moral Majority and similar groups are part of a coalition formed with elements of the older far Right at a meeting held December 19, 1978, in Washington. This was a very carefully thought out meeting which laid the groundwork for the tactics of the right-wingers in the 1980 election. The members of the older Right, that had been ejected by the electorate in the Goldwater campaign of 1964, sensed that the American Evangelical movement had shifted to the Right from its historical position of Christian concern for the abolition of slavery, the growth of public education, and the rights of women (all part of the Evangelical revival of the nineteenth century).[7] The Evangelical movement was fascinated by a media preaching that was hostile to public education, rejective of women's rights, and critical of welfare recipients. Right-wing political planners were struck by the tremendous possibilities of exploiting this Evangelical movement as a means to achieving the political power they had been denied in previous elections.

Greene describes a little-understood background of the electronic religion that the church desperately needs to expose. Ironically, the roots of the Moral Majority message go back to the traumas of the great divisions between Americans in the Civil War period. The tactics of a form of evangelism which grew out of the defeated South have been appropriated by these right-wing religionists, many of whom, not coincidentally, are Southerners. Feelings of hatred and bitterness growing out of the Civil War and Reconstruction periods produced a negative religion which preached divine vengeance against a "godless" North. Now the right wing preaches against "godless" communism. While lynching of blacks is no longer sanctioned from the pulpit, minority groups are seen as nonproductive drains on the system. Enemies of a particular socioeconomic order are consigned to hell.[8]

We have scholarly evidence that the journalist Greene is sound in his insight that there is a Southern connection in the message of the new religious Right that goes far beyond the Southern origins of many of the evangelists.

In discussing the controversies of Fundamentalism and Liberalism in an earlier day, George M. Marsden, professor of history at Calvin College, observes:

> In the South the debates were in most cases short-lived, because dissent was simply not tolerated. As early as the first half of the nineteenth century, advanced theological views had usually been associated with advanced social views and abolition. Southern theology already had a strong conservative bent. The War Between the States simply intensified Southern determination to resist change. Hence there was a strong anti-modernist impulse in Southern religion well before modernism became a distinct movement in America. This theological conservatism, often combined with the warm revivalist evangelicalism inherited from the early nineteenth century . . . resembled later fundamentalism. Until the 1920s, however, Southern revivalist conservatism and Northern fundamentalism developed more or less independently, although in parallel ways. The principal direct connection between the two movements was that several important fundamentalist leaders came from the South. When in the twentieth century fundamentalism became a distinct entity, Southerners with a long history of revivalist conservatism eventually flocked to the movement.[9]

Marsden goes on to discuss the breakdown of Fundamentalism after 1925. What he says about the 1920s is worth recording because

97

it sounds so similar to the many charges of conspiracies, struggle against public education, the conflict over the teaching of evolution, and even the Ku Klux Klan activity which characterize the present day. The message of the religious Right today is strangely similar to the last cries of a dying Fundamentalism fifty-five years ago. Marsden observes:

"For the first time in our history," declared Maynard Shipley in his *War on Modern Science*, appearing the same year, "organized knowledge has come into open conflict with organized ignorance." . . . Fundamentalists across the country had been organizing vociferous, anti-evolution lobbies under the leadership of such organizations as the World's Christian Fundamentals Association and the related Anti-evolution League. George F. Washburn, a friend of Bryan's, although not previously an active fundamentalist, proclaimed himself "the successor of William Jennings Bryan." He founded the Bible Crusaders of America, including a number of fundamentalist leaders to join the fight "Back to Christ, the Bible, and the Constitution." Other friends of Bryan undertook massive money-raising drives, with the intention of creating a William Jennings Bryan University. Meanwhile, in California, evangelist Paul W. Rood reported a vision from God calling *him* to be Bryan's successor, which led to the formation of the Bryan Bible League. Next, Gerald Winrod of Kansas founded the Defenders of the Christian Faith, another organization using the methods of sensationalism to fight evolution and modernism. Winrod sent a squadron of "flying fundamentalists" through the Midwest and elsewhere to promote the anti-evolution cause. Edgar Young Clark, a former national organizer for the Ku Klux Klan, attempted to cash in on this trend with the foundation of the Supreme Kingdom, which was structured like the Klan but had fundamentalist anti-modernist and anti-evolutionary goals.[10]

We are indebted to Marsden for giving us the resources to identify the continuity of the right-wing attack in the ongoing interplay of religion and social issues.

I must repeat that getting clear about facts is only the groundwork for the church's work in developing a healthier faith in the people of our society. When I get to some suggestions of strategies that might be used to promote healthy religion, I will be mentioning other resources, such as the writings of Professor Karl Popper, that help to analyze the political theories that lie behind right-wing movements. But meanwhile the church's task is to change attitudes, and conveying information is only a part of this task.

It seems to me that there are six elements that go into the church's development of a healthier form of faith. How these elements can be made effective lies in the realm of practice and experimentation. The suggestions made here are only meant as guides. Each local church will have to work out methods of its own that effect attitudinal changes in the people it serves.

The elements of healthy faith are:

1. Development of a taste for freedom—freedom of inquiry and freedom of responsible decision making among church people and others that one can influence.

2. The continual stress of the prophetic element in religion—the proclamation that God is not served by ceremony and platitude but by love and justice in human relations. The element of condemnation of human practices that is part of the prophetic message must be balanced by the equally prophetic word of grace and the promise of pardon to those who repent. Above all, the church must not allow the prophetic message of the Bible to be misused by presentation in a one-sided manner that makes it punitive and vengeful. The church must not glory in the ability to condemn others while not holding out the promise of pardon. The prophetic element must always be truly biblical in that the judgment against human attitudes and practices must begin, in Peter's phrase, in the house of God itself. The church can never be a serious, godly critic of the people and society if it is not first a critic of itself. The church must continually reform itself by the light of its own prophetic witness. It is the self-satisfied smugness of the Moral Majority which holds that some people are moral while others are not that shows its proclamations to be unbiblical. This is a one-sided, thinly disguised form of self-worship. On this basis we can understand the condemnation of Jerry Falwell, Pat Robertson, and others by the groups called "People for the American Way" and the leaders of fifteen of the largest Protestant denominations. These groups condemn the Evangelical Right as theologically, biblically, and politically unsound. Anything that is less than the whole counsel of God is surely unsound.

3. The church must promote emotional growth and encourage integrity in character development. This sounds like a strange thing to say, for surely all religious education has this ideal as one of its aims. Nonetheless, emotional growth toward maturity is not characteristic of many human beings in churches. Integrity of

character remains an ideal for many of us. Obviously, it is nonsense to speak of sanctification in the theological sense as a possible characteristic of a believer who has not emotionally matured and is not moving toward self-integrity. Nevertheless, much of the preaching and moralizing of conservative religious leaders and teachers is a retarding element in human emotional growth. Here is where a strategy to promote healthy faith presents itself. It is not some new media technique, nor is it the use of an exotic psychology. The strategy that can help promote emotional growth on a mass basis is preaching itself. Preaching that encourages dependency, that recommends rigid doctrinaire thinking, and worst of all, that is basically hostile toward society at large and subgroups in that society, is actually promoting emotional immaturity. In the theological sense it is calling evil good, promoting sin in the name of morality. The preaching of those who have won a warm reception because they have been against the movements and events that the very conservative groups are against must be countered by preaching that promotes honesty in analyzing the social situation, that is prophetic in its stress on ethics, and that promotes positive emotional growth toward maturity.

The element of dependency should be clarified. The "star system" of preaching to millions of people and by this means acquiring not only great sources of wealth and political influence but also acquiring the charisma and projected strength of celebrity status, ultimately reduces the electronic congregation to followers of one undisputed leader. The charisma and personal power of the electronic preacher become similar to the charismatic, singular authority of the cult leader. The rise of Jim Jones from popular preacher to unquestioned cult leader to one who equated himself with God should give us a disturbing example of what can be the result of preaching that encourages dependency. No person should be able to say, as Falwell has said, that he can "deliver five million votes." One has to ask, "Where is the prophetic or priestly role in such an activity?"

4. Such preaching by the churches must also promote intellectual growth and integrity, which will be major in making the *actual* religious-political scene clear to as many people as can be reached. This means we must move beyond preaching in the local

congregation to public preaching, perhaps in rallies, which the conservatives have long used, and move boldly into television and radio. The promotion of the truth cannot be limited to parish pulpits. The media cannot be abandoned to the sole use of those who are using them for the acquisition of power.

Part of this truth telling, unfortunately, must include the revealing of the roots of the Moral Majority message, a clear delineation of its departure from biblical and theological norms, and presentations of the psychological characteristics of the authoritarian personality as part of the promotion of emotional growth. This will reveal the feet of clay that many of the new Right preachers and organizations have. This is unfortunate because it is never easy, nor is it usually right, for Christians to point out the shortcomings of others. Nonetheless, the truth must be told.

Interestingly enough, the news magazines have done more to present facts about the ordinary humanity of the popular preachers than any other agency. The magazine *Newsweek* (which is surely not a liberal publication) reported on September 15, 1980, that Jerry Falwell's Thomas Road Baptist Church was sued by the Securities and Exchange Commission for issuing allegedly fraudulent bonds.[11] Reportedly, he borrows from his college fund to pay his media costs. As is the case with many of the electronic evangelists, there is no clear-cut accounting of how much money Falwell raises or for what purposes it is used. The Better Business Bureau criticizes Falwell for that.[12] One thing is certain: Falwell seems to have all of the millions of dollars that flow in to him working in one or the other of his many projects so that raising money is a full-time activity. Without this continuous calling for funds, Falwell's empire would probably fall apart.[13]

We should not overlook the fact that Falwell was not above lying about an official as high as the President of the United States. Johnny Greene recounts an incident that took place before the 1980 election at an Alaska gathering where Falwell misrepresented a previous meeting he had had with Mr. Carter. Falwell quoted a conversation in which he asked Carter point blank why he had homosexuals on his senior staff at the White House. When the White House transcript revealed that the conversation had never taken place, Falwell's explanation was:

"I have stated as clearly and emphatically as I know how that my recent statement was not intended to be a verbatim report of our conversation with President Carter.

"Instead, my statement was intended to be, and was, an honest portrayal of President Carter's position on gay rights. It was an anecdote, intended to dramatically get the attention of the audience. It was an accurate statement of the President's record and position on gay rights. It was meant to be nothing else."[14]

I find it difficult to believe in the moral pronouncements of someone who can stretch the truth in such a manner. But what is more frightening is the realization that these kinds of moral lapses seem to be indicative of a complete lack of integrity on the part of the person. One has to ask then how much of the rest of the religious proclamation and political analysis of such a person is also out of touch with reality and possibly a tissue of lies? One slip may not condemn a personality, but unfortunately, in religion, it has the blasphemous effect of calling into question the truth of the religious teaching itself.

5. The church must expand its mandate to preach the gospel and uphold morals to recognize also that it has the duty to promote logical thinking. This does not mean thinking along one set line, nor does it mean the teaching of a "Christian philosophy." It means standing up for the rights of the social sciences and physical sciences to investigate whatever these disciplines see as necessary, without hindrance from those who would suppress knowledge out of fear of change.

The church must support logical thinking about the social involvements of the church and its members. Above all, support must be mobilized to defend the public school system which is now under attack from the religious Right even more severely than the universities were attacked by the conservatives during the 1960s and 1970s. This does not mean that the church may not criticize society, the sciences, or the schools, but it does mean that the church cannot be allowed to intimidate or attempt to control scientific research or education. There is plenty of room for ethical analysis in biomedical matters, in law, and in methods of teaching, without resorting to intimidation. The hobbyhorses of the far Right must be criticized and opposed by the mainstream churches. Votes must be mobilized on school boards and at the ballot box when attempts are made to attack biologists for teaching evolution. Special creationism should be opposed on the simple grounds that something which is a matter of faith for believers cannot be made a matter of scientific truth for nonbelievers. We cannot allow religion to be spread by force, even if that force is one at the ballot box. God is not worshiped by the misuse of his creatures. If the Christian faith is true, it needs no special pleading. We cannot allow our intellectuals to suffer a twentieth-century version of Galileo's trials. The churches have the heaviest obligation to label clearly, in detail, the heretical unorthodox interpretations of the Bible that form the core of Fundamentalist belief. To allow those who oppose evolution and promote creationism to infer that theirs is a proper interpretation of Scripture is to promote heresy silently. We have an example for what the churches at large might do in the action by moderates in the Lutheran Church-Missouri Synod, who heroically defied attempts by Fundamentalists to make creationism an article of faith. The moderates founded the Association of Evangelical Lutheran Churches and Christ Seminary. They clearly pointed out that nothing in the history of the universal Christian church, nor any article of the orthodox creeds or confessions, implied that the Fundamentalist view on Genesis is orthodox. The church at large must show the same courage and make its stand publicly known.

While emotional distortions of logic are questions to be treated by psychologists and involve attitudes and feelings more than errors of knowledge, nevertheless, the churches have the duty to point out the illogical character of the various conspiracy theories promoted by both the religious and political Right. The fact that scholars show that earlier Fundamentalism also included such conspiracy theories, that the "paranoid style in politics" of the McCarthy era was founded on conspiracy theories, that worldwide anti-Semitism that ended in the holocaust death of six million Jews was buttressed by a falacious conspiracy theory based on the spurious Protocols of the Elders of Zion, and that such false documents still circulate among the Ku Klux Klan, should make us aware of the danger of paranoid thinking. The fact that the present religious right wing also operates on a conspiracy-theory basis, having substituted the vague term "secular humanism" for "Jews" or "Communists," and that much was said during the 1980 election about the "tri-lateral commission" as a supposed center of conspiracy, should warn us that paranoia in political and religious thinking must be opposed lest we be brought again to bloodshed and tragedy.

6. It is the business of genuine religion to be redemptive, to heal, to bind together, and to oppose that which separates, hurts, and defames other people. The church must redeem the words and ideas that have been wantonly and falsely made negative in much of the public's mind. We have a duty to promote a pluralistic, open society of individual liberty in which the freedom to believe according to one's own conscience is respected and guaranteed. We must redeem the word "secular," not so hard to do since it is a theological word in any case. It is possible to show that the "secular" itself is a creation of the Christian church, a distancing of the sacred rites and powers of the church from the general affairs of man in the city of man, by the creation of, in Luther's words, two kingdoms, or in Augustine's words, two cities. The kingdom of the state or the realm of the secular, the city of man, is God-founded just as is the city of God, the realm of the church or the sacred. Both areas have their own integrity, and neither is to be supreme over the other. That which is the rule in the church cannot be made the rule in the state. That which is necessary for salvation cannot be made necessary for citizenship. Just as we would have to fight to preserve the rights of the church to be free of secular control, even so we must fight to insure that the state is free of the church's control. Although they were not theologians and most were not orthodox Christians, the founding fathers of the United States were in agreement with the concept of the two kingdoms. Separation of church and state is not just an idea; it is and it must be kept a fact. Theological distinctions cannot be allowed room in that realm where God allows people to exercise their natural powers. The Fundamentalists need to think about this very seriously; for if it is possible to create a civil disability for a liberal or an atheist or a homosexual, then it is equally possible for a civil disability to be created for a Fundamentalist who may not believe some exotic doctrine. Once we begin to separate the sheep from the goats on this, the historical side of the final judgment, then there is no logical place to stop drawing the line. Ultimately more and more people will be judged tainted until the pure are a small ruling elite or, more likely, only one man is good and right and exercises all power. "Judge not that ye be not judged" is a passage of Scripture that biblicists need to seek to understand.

We must redeem the word "humanism"; for humanism is the product of the Judeo-Christian culture. Humanism in its best sense is a kind of open outlook on life and the world that has moved beyond prejudice, racism, and other limits of the human spirit. Of course, it is possible to be a humanist and an agnostic, or even an atheist, but this does not by any means imply that humanism is agnostic or atheistic. Humanism, even in the agnostic, remains at least a para-religious outlook, since the foundations of humanism lie in the Renaissance with its secularizing of much classical religious and Christian belief. We must defend the humanities and the humanistic impulse and promote a godly humanism that fosters belief in truth, compassion for people, and the ability to tolerate ambiguity. This is only to say that we must attempt to recover a genuinely humane way of looking at society and its problems, for unfortunately it is precisely the humane impulses in the social legislation of previous administrations that the religious Right detests and seems to want to destroy. This cannot be combated with soft words; we must expose the errors of right-wing logic and recapture the noble words and concepts that they have maliciously distorted. This can only be done by prophetic preaching and massive persuasion by way of the media.

6

Strategies to Promote Healthy Religion

It is not easy to discover strategies to deal effectively with perversions of political and religious ideas. Yet we have numerous such perversions in the contemporary world to deal with. Besides the great bulk of the Moral Majority Evangelicals the church also has scores of religious cults that need to be combated with logic, truth, and persuasion. The question remains, how?

Thinking About Strategies

The problem in devising strategy is further complicated by the fact that those who have perverted religious ideas have been the keenest observers of the modern scene and have gained early access to the most powerful tools of communication, radio and television. Indeed, the electronic church has a virtual monopoly on national television, both because of the lack of foresight of the mainstream denominations and because of the vast amounts of money needed to operate such projects. Falwell, Robertson, and others regularly take in more millions of dollars than whole denominations do. Then these millions are poured back into the mass media again. There seems to be no way that a church denomination can keep up with that. Christian denominations and Jewish groups operate colleges and seminaries, hospitals and schools, give vast amounts of money to the relief of suffering, and do extensive publication, besides extending their beliefs through missions. The percentage of the income of such legitimate denominations that can be *channelled* into mass media is limited. The electronic church has no such restrictions on its work. The television evangelists give money to no one, do not support a denominational system of seminaries and schools—although each evangelist may build his own school or hospital as in the case of Falwell or Oral Roberts—rather the money they receive they keep and use to expand their empires continually.

Nevertheless, one of the basic strategies that mainstream churches must adopt to promote healthy religion should be a dedication to capturing a portion of national television and radio time. Something more than the denominational programs—as good as some of them are—that are presently undertaken must be developed. Preachers and other personalities who can attract the masses can be and must be discovered and developed. We must find the proper physical vehicles that can draw the attention of the public and then stress the need for an open society and challenge the religious Right to debate. Truth must oppose error, and humane compassion must be presented as the Christian alternative to sectarian separatism and judgmentalism.

This will not be possible unless it is done by a general, concerted effort by all denominations. Only the Roman Catholic Church would have the strength to oppose the electronic church; and since we wish to promote a pluralistic, open society for all forms of faith and life, it would not be desirable for one communion to take on the battle alone. But since conservatism in our period is the expression of a general social disorientation that is characteristic of Europe as well as America, there may be problems here, as conservative thinking and actions are growing more frequent in the post-Vatican II Roman Catholic Church. This may make ecumenical cooperation between Catholics, Protestants, and Jews slightly more difficult than it has been for the last decade. Nevertheless, there is a real climate of cooperation and openness toward Judaism. We must build on these feelings and extend them, for only a concerted effort by all three of the genuine forms of biblical faith in our country will be able to generate the financial power, the influence, and prestige that would be needed to combat the religious and political Right.

Part of the religious programming projected here should involve scholarship in the history of ideas and in the history of Christianity and Judaism. We must sponsor scholarship and then also insist, contrary to the present practice, that scholarship be translated into popular form, not only in books but also through the electronic media as well. Studies such as those made by Karl R. Popper in *The Open Society and Its Enemies, volumes 1 and 2*[1] need to be communicated to the public. Indeed, Popper's book deals with the philosophical and theological basis of the radical right position, calling it the dogma of the closed society. Popper identifies this dogma as "the taboo theory of politics." According to this theory, the ideal society is governed in accordance with canons that are exempted from criticism. When one thinks of the myth of a righteous Christian America and a belief that God will protect it from all its enemies, along with the belief that something called the free enterprise system is in accord with God's will and not to be questioned, we can see that the Moral Majority promotes the taboo theory in a classical form.

The taboo theory holds that it is wicked for people to try to change society. Too much intellectualism is also wicked, for to philosophize and reflect on our human experience is dangerous. It is as the Reverend Robert Billings, president of the National Christian Action Coalition and the executive director of Moral Majority says: "People want leadership. They don't know what to think themselves. They want to be told what to think by those of us here close to the front."[2]

What the leaders of the Moral Majority are describing is precisely the taboo theory of political life, a magical or irrational attitude toward the customs of social life and a rigidity in demand that those customs be followed. This is the tribal or primitive way of life followed in the earliest days of civilization. It was this kind of society that Plato wished to set up in Athens and described in detail in the *Republic*. Plato was willing to admit that, in order to get such a state going, a great lie must be told, the lie of racism, that there are different kinds of men, of which only a few are fitted by God or nature to rule.

Plato's *Republic* was the historical model for Mussolini's fascism, and the concept of the single ruler of a racially pure society which Plato develops is the ideological ancestor of Nazism with its "führer principle" and its concept of a master race. We need to be very wary of closed societies.

The closed society is often described as an organism. This is the biological theory of the state as the fatherland or the motherland, in which society represents a herd or tribe in that it is a semiorganic unit held together by biological ties of race and kinship. Interestingly enough, Mussolini refers to fascism as the organic theory of the state.

It is worth quoting Mussolini, in that he was one dictator who attempted to make sense out of what he believed.

> *Facism is a religious conception* in which man is seen in his immanent relationship with a superior law and with an objective Will that transcends the particular individual and raises him to conscious membership of a spiritual society. Whoever has seen in the religious politics of the Fascist regime nothing but mere opportunism has not understood that Fascism besides being a system of government is also, and above all, a system of thought.
>
> *Fascism is a historical conception,* in which man is what he is only in so far as he works with the spiritual process in which he finds himself in the family or social group, in the nation and in the history in which all nations collaborate. From this follows the great value of tradition, in memories, in language, in customs, in the standards of social life.[3]

Interestingly enough, just as the right wing today is opposed to socialism and often criticizes the concept of democracy, claiming that the United States is a republic and not a democracy, Mussolini rejected and despised socialism, labor unions, and democracy. Mussolini wrote:

> Outside the State there can be neither individuals nor groups (political parties, associations, syndicates, classes). Therefore Fascism is opposed to Socialism, which confines the movement of history within the class struggle and ignores the unity of classes established in one economic and moral reality in the State; and analogously it is opposed to class syndicalism [labor unions]. Fascism recognizes the real exigencies for which the socialist and syndicalist movement arose, but while recognizing them wishes to bring them under the control of the State and give them a purpose within the corporative system of interests reconciled within the unity of the State.[4]

Of course, the great mass of people who have been attracted to the religious Right are not in sympathy with fascism. One of the myths about the right wing that the church's strategy of teaching must combat is the claim that the right wing is monolithic. It is not. Just as the so-called Evangelical movement is made up of dozens of different denominations, sects, and para-church agencies, the political Right is made up of many different organizations and groups of voters. Without doubt, the Ku Klux Klan and neo-Nazi types compose only a very tiny minority of the people on the Right. The problem that we must point out is that the teachings of the Right are not democratic, and their religious views are not those of orthodox Christianity. The Right, unfortunately, creates a climate in which the seedy elements of fascism become more respectable than they otherwise would be. This is the danger that must be pointed up.

The church must mount an attack upon the resurgent racism that is beginning to appear. Not to speak out against this makes us silent accessories to the inhumanity perpetuated by racist groups.

In turning to the "conspiracy theories" so prominent on the Right, we should remember that Hitler had no problem in convincing the German veterans of World War I that they had not been defeated on the battlefield but had been betrayed by an international conspiracy of Jewish bankers. We also need to remember that a similar theory of General MacArthur's being sold out by the administration in Washington was put forward by many conservatives as the reason why United Nations forces ended the Korean conflict in a stalemate with the Communist forces. The Vietnam struggle, with its undoubted defeat of the United States and its South Vietnamese allies, is widely understood as the result of the refusal of the United States government to try really to win that conflict. America is the playground for many conspiracy theories, and the hostilities engendered by this magical form of thinking explain much of the voting support gathered together by the right wing in the 1980 election.

Attempting to make public in a clear manner the fallacies in the thinking and message of the right wing could go far toward overcoming the lack of understanding on the part of the electorate. The exposure of the magical or irrational nature of conspiracy theories would also do much to cope with the pessimism and fear that seem to be reflected in many citizens.

Conspiracy theories have played a large part in American life since World War II. The rise to national prominence by Richard Nixon was partially accomplished by Nixon's role in the McCarthy era with its conspiracy theory of international communism. The Alger Hiss case and other public identifications of Nixon as a strong anti-Communist helped to give him the support that years later would lead him to the White House. The assassination of President Kennedy led to a whole host of conspiracy theories. Interestingly enough, in December, 1980, a government committee found that there was evidence on audiotapes made at the time of the assassination that there were unaccounted-for shots that pointed to conspiracy. No less an agency than the FBI disputed these findings, showing that the same manner of interpretation followed by the committee could lead to absurd consequences.

How cunningly an authoritarian program can be hidden in the apparently innocent desire of Christian people is revealed by Johnny Greene in his discussion of the Family Protection Act. Ostensibly the supporters of this act are promoting the interests of the American family. Yet by manipulation of such an emotional issue—by suggesting, for example, the legislation of prayer in public schools—they threaten the doctrines of separation of church and state and separation of powers, potentially weakening our governmental system.[5]

It is important that we make the public aware of the thinking of these right-wing leaders. There is more to their program than meets the eye.

Accentuate the Positive

There are many human assets on the side of reaction, the call to return to the past. There is something in human beings who are not authoritarian but only sentimental and idealistic that responds to a call to defend the old religion. These good elements in people have again and again been misused, from the Spartans (who cultivated allies even in Athens during the Peloponnesian War), to Hitler, to the latest orator proclaiming the need to make the old-time religion real again. So it is easy to say that we should develop a taste for freedom in people, defuse racial, sexual, and ethnic prejudices, and promote intellectual growth and integrity. How do we do this? This is particularly difficult when pluralism, the presence of many beliefs and many different life-styles, is a major part of the social situation that disturbs the millions drawn by the message of the religious Right. How can we develop a taste for a pluralistic society in the minds and feelings of middle America?

The only obvious answer is by education, by a long-term process of analyzing and describing the events of history that have brought us to the place in which we stand. And this presents a problem within a problem, for it is the expressed wish of the Right to curb such an education and promote its own brand of education in its so-called Christian schools. One of the strategies of the main-line churches must be a stout educational and legal defense of public education. Along with this must go a defense of the constitutional separation of church and state. We must expose the right-wing conception of the state as a religious entity and of the political leader as the guardian of morals. It is precisely the attack on the American system that allows us the warrant to wage a political battle in the name of freedom against the right-wing onslaught.

The difference between magical or tribal thinking, that believes blindly that problems can be solved by one grand vote or act of punishment of the conspirators, and a real-world, healthy understanding of life, is partly that the rational outlook knows that solutions to problems take time. If we have problems, and indeed we do, it may take as long to solve those problems as it took to get ourselves into them. One of the Christian virtues surely is patience. Again, without underwriting *or* denying the goodness or desirability of various social movements and life-styles, such as feminism and homosexuality, the church can and should stress the Christian virtue of charity. Tolerance is but the political manifestation of the family orientation of charity or love. A concerted attack in love (ironically) on the punitive spirit that is searching for scapegoats for the relative loss of power of the United States in the world since World War II, and for the energy crisis, must be made. Even in cases where bad judgment has been employed in social policy or where genuine malfactors exist, as in the case of those who misuse the welfare system, we must point out the Christian virtue of forgiveness. Perhaps the most progressive thing the main-line church could do would be to return to the old-fashioned basics of preaching clearly about the Christian virtues—which are similar to Jewish and Muslim virtues—that make life together possible, tolerable, and enjoyable.

There is reason to believe that such preaching and teaching can find a receptive ear among millions of people attracted to the religious Right, for there is no reason to believe that religious belief is not sincere in many of them. We have, too, the studies of Alan C. Elms in his *Social Psychology and Social Relevance*,[6] who studied people attracted to the right wing from the 1940s through the early 1970s. Elms found that American rightists did not correlate well with the authoritarian personality syndrome identified by Adorno.

Rather, he found most right-wingers, including members of the John Birch Society, to be psychologically healthy and well adjusted. He found, in studying a number of people in the Dallas, Texas, area who were quite active in Birch Society activities, that these people had become right-wingers because of socialization rather than out of any psychological problems. Living in a community where the media was dominated by right-wing views and such attitudes were socially acceptable, such people got social payoffs in acceptance for holding such views.

Elms, in a prophetic insight, says that future right-wing movements will gain their strength from such socialized right-wingers rather than from malcontents and rigidly authoritarian individuals. This certainly seems true and seems to be a good explanation for what happened in the November, 1980, election. The electronic church and the Moral Majority mailings and meetings socialized people into right-wing opinions. What only a few people would say earlier, the preachers said to millions and made it respectable. This is a shame, but it is also the key to how the church, through the same intense kind of proclamation, can remind Christians and people of goodwill of the basic religious virtues. Perhaps we can make racial tolerance, forbearance, forgiveness, and patience respectable again. We can oppose the law of punishment with the law of love. I do not believe that love has lost any of its power to redeem, to reunite, to save, and to heal.

Appendix A

A Summary of the Provisions of the Proposed Family Protection Act

The following is a brief summary of the provisions of S. 1808 (96th Congress, first session), a bill "to strengthen the American family and promote the virtues of family life through education, tax assistance, and related measures." The bill was introduced by Senator Paul Laxalt in June, 1979. It is commonly called the "Family Protection Act." This piece of suggested legislation represents the political purposes of the Moral Majority movement.

Preamble

The Family Protection Act states that "a stable and healthy American family is at the foundation of a strong American society." It goes on to say that "the Government has frequently fostered policies which undermine the viability of the American family, through its policies of taxation and spending." The Act intends ". . . to remove those Federal Governmental policies" which inhibit the family's strength and prosperity.

Title I—Education

No federal funds will be given a state that prohibits voluntary prayer in any public building. Procedures must be in place so that parents and community representatives can be part of decisions on courses relating to religion. Parental consent must be given for students to take such courses. Classes and records must be open to parental inspection. School districts can't require teachers to pay dues (i.e., union dues, NEA dues).

Parents must be able to review textbooks before class use. No programs "seeking to inculcate values or modes of behavior which contradict the demonstrated beliefs and values of the community" or "deny the role differences between the sexes" are allowed.

Certification requirements are loosened, as are attendance requirements (they may be abolished), and the intermingling of the sexes in school-related activities may be prohibited, all without loss of federal funds.

Families may set up savings plans for education and deduct the amounts contributed from their income tax, up to $2,500 per year. There will be no taxes on such accounts.

Title XI—Elementary and Secondary School Assistance Program

Unconditional educational grants will be made to the states and to *local* educational agencies of $4,500,000,000 for the fiscal year 1981 and for each year up to October 1, 1984. Each state will receive an amount in ratio to the number of children in each state, age five to seventeen inclusive, who are enrolled in public schools. Funds shall not be used to build facilities for worship or religious instruction, but released time for parenthood education conducted by churches—and in fulfillment of required courses—is allowed. Discrimination is forbidden, but a court must prove that a school intentionally discriminated for at least four consecutive years prior to the filing of the suit.

Title II—Welfare

Credits up to $1,000 against income taxes are given to those who care for elderly or disabled dependents. College students are forbidden to participate in the food stamp program. No agency may require licensing or regulate a day-care center.

Title III—First Amendment Guarantees

Religious institutions (day-care centers, foster homes, and others) are exempt from any federal regulations.

Title IV—Taxation

Married couples are given income tax advantages over single persons. Persons in religious and civic activities on a voluntary basis (i.e., wives) are counted as gainfully employed, for income tax purposes.

Each child born to or adopted by a taxpayer gives an exemption of $1,000 and for adoption of mixed-race children, $3,000 (this deduction can be carried over from year to year).

Trusts to benefit parents or handicapped relatives may be set up, with $3,000 tax-free contributions.

Title V—Domestic Relations

Federal programs are not to alter existing state laws on child abuse or to establish child abuse programs in states unless requested. "Child abuse" is *not* to include discipline or corporal punishment methods by parents or individuals authorized by parents. Federal programs are not to alter existing state laws on spousal abuse or domestic relations. Contraceptive devices or information are not to be given to unmarried minors unless parents are notified. The same applies to abortion counseling and the treatment of venereal disease. Parents of minors must be informed of all these occurrences. Legal aid is also forbidden as an outgrowth of federal programs.

No federal funds may be given to any public or private individual or groups that present male or female homosexuality as an acceptable life-style or that suggest "unlawful employment practices" be modified to exclude discrimination against homosexuals or those who defend them.

Any person who violates any provision of the act is subject to a civil penalty of $5,000 for each violation, each day of a continuing offense constituting a separate violation.

Appendix B

Family Issues Voting Index

Ten votes in the House and Senate that the National Christian Action Coalition felt had a definite pro- or anti- family implication were selected. These votes date back to summer, 1977. Each member's *rating* was computed by dividing the number of *plus* votes by the total number of votes recorded. This was prepared by the National Christian Action Coalition through the Christian Voters' Victory Fund.

Senate votes recorded and rated include:

1. Abortion (H.R. 7555) (NAY–plus)
2. School Busing (S. 1753) (NAY–plus)
3. School Prayer Amendment (S. 210) (NAY–plus)
4. Sex Education (66 S. 210) (YEA–plus)
5. Education Department (S. 210) (NAY–plus)
6. ERA Deadline Extension (H.J. Res 638) (NAY–plus)
7. Wald Nomination (July 24, 1979) (NAY–plus)
8. IRS and Private Schools (H.R. 4393) (NAY–plus)
9. Fiscal 1980 Binding Budget Level (290 S. Con Res 36) (YEA–plus)
10. Child Welfare and Social Services (H.R. 3434) (YEA–plus)

House votes recorded and rated include:

1. Abortion (H.R. 7555) (YEA–plus)
2. IRS and Private Schools (H.R. 4393) (YEA–plus)
3. Creation of a Cabinet—Level Education Department (H.R. 2444) (NAY–plus)

4. School Busing (H.R. 7555) (YEA–plus)
5. Equal Rights Amendment (H.J. Res 638) (NAY–plus)
6. Homosexual Rights (H.R. 6666) (YEA–plus)
7. Domestic Violence (passed December 12, 1979) (NAY–plus)
8. Prayer in Public Schools (H.R. 2444) (YEA–plus)
9. Child Health Assurance Act of 1979 (H.R. 4962) (NAY–plus)
10. Inflation Fighter/Balance Budget (H. Con Res. 107) (YEA–plus)

The booklet then goes on to rate the members of the House and Senate. As mentioned in the text, Richard Kelly, Republican congressman from Florida, received a rating of 100 and was convicted in the ABSCAM trials in January, 1981.

Notes

Chapter 1

[1]John C. Cooper, *The Turn Right* (Philadelphia: The Westminster Press, 1970).

[2]John C. Cooper, *Religion in the Age of Aquarius* (Philadelphia: The Westminister Press, 1971).

[3]Sinclair Lewis, *It Can't Happen Here* (New York: Doubleday & Co., Inc., 1935).

[4]John C. Cooper, "Extreme Danger," *The Lutheran* (May 6, 1981), p. 5.

[5]John C. Cooper, *The Recovery of America* (Philadelphia: The Westminster Press, 1973).

[6]Harry and Bonaro Overstreet, *The Strange Tactics of Extremism* (New York: W.W. Norton & Co., Inc., 1964).

[7]Associated Press news story.

[8]James M. Wall, "The New Right Comes of Age," *The Christian Century* (October 22, 1980), p. 996.

[9]Gerald R. Gill, *The Manness Mania: The Changed Mood* (Washington, D. C.: Howard University Press, 1980).

[10]Faustine Childress Jones, *The Changing Mood in America: Eroding Commitment?* (Washington, D. C.: Howard University Press, 1977) p. viii.

[11]*Ibid.*, p. 23.

[12]Rodney Stark and Charles Y. Glock, *Christian Beliefs and Anti-Semitism* (New York: Harper & Row, Publishers, Inc., 1966). See also *American Piety-The Nature of Religious Commitment* (Berkeley, Calif.: University of California Press, 1968) by the same authors.

[13]Doug and Bill Wead, *Reagan in Pursuit of the Presidency—1980* (Plainfield, N. J.: Logos International, 1980).

[14]M. Searle Bates, *Religious Liberty: An Inquiry* (New York: International Missionary Council, 1945).

[15]D. G. Kehl, "Peddling the Power and the Promises," *Christianity Today* (March 21, 1980), pp. 16ff.

[16]Homer Duncan, *Secular Humanism* (Lubbock, Tex.: Missionary Crusader, 1979).

[17]Jurgen Moltmann, *The Crucified God* (New York: Harper & Row, Publishers, Inc., 1974), p. 318.

Chapter 2

[1]"Reagan Endorses Call to 'Old-Time Religion'" *The Lutheran* (September 17, 1980), p. 18.
[2]Greg Denier, "A Shift Toward the Right? Or a Failure of the Left?" *Christianity and Crisis*, vol. 40, no. 21 (December 22, 1980), pp. 355-360.
[3]Harry and Bonaro Overstreet, *The Strange Tactics of Extremism* (New York: W.W. Norton & Co., Inc., 1964), p. 208.
[4]George J. Church, "Politics from the Pulpit," *Time* (October 13, 1980), p. 35. Reprinted by permission from TIME, The Weekly Newsmagazine; Copyright Time, Inc., 1980.
[5]Interview with Tim LaHaye in *The Wittenberg Door*, no. 55 (June/July, 1980), pp. 9-10.
[6]Overstreet, *op. cit.*, pp. 144-145.
[7]*Ibid.*, p. 33.
[8]*The Wittenberg Door*, op. cit., p. 12.
[9]*Ibid.*
[10]*Ibid.*, pp. 10, 15.
[11]*Ibid*, p. 15.

Chapter 3

[1]Dean Kelley, *Why Conservative Churches Are Growing* (New York: Harper & Row, Publishers, Inc., 1972), p. 84. See Chart D: "Strong" and "Weak" Groups.
[2]*Ibid*, p. 85.
[3]*Ibid*, p. 84.
[4]*Ibid.*
[5]*Ibid.*
[6]*Ibid.*
[7]*Ibid.*
[8]"Born Again at the Ballot Box," *Time* (April 14, 1980), p. 94.
[9]"Getting God's Kingdom into Politics," *Christianity Today* (September 19, 1980), pp. 10-11. Copyright © 1980 by *Christianity Today*. Used by permission.
[10]*Toledo Blade* (September 21, 1980), section B, p. 3. Reprinted by permission from *The Blade*, Toledo, Ohio.
[11]*Ibid.*
[12]Robert Zwier and Richard Smith, "Christian Politics and the New Right," *The Christian Century* (October 9, 1980), p. 940. Copyright 1980 Christian Century Foundation. Reprinted by permission.
[13]*Ibid.*, pp. 939-940.
[14]Jerry Falwell, *Listen, America* (New York: Galilee Books, imprint of Doubleday & Co., Inc., 1980), p. 135.
[15]*Ibid.*, pp. 136-137.
[16]James M. Wall, "The New Right Comes of Age," *The Christian Century*

(October 22, 1980), p. 996. Copyright 1980 Christian Century Foundation. Reprinted by permission.

[17]Martin Marty, "Points to Consider About the New Christian Right Wing," *The Wittenberg Door*, no. 55 (June/July, 1980) p. 26. Originally appeared in the July 15, 1980, issue of *Context*. Reprinted from *Context* by permission of Claretian Publications, 221 West Madison, Chicago, IL 60606.

[18]*Ibid.*, p. 27.

[19]*Ibid.*, pp. 27-28.

Chapter 4

[1]Robert N. Bellah and Philip E. Hammond, *Varieties of Civil Religion* (New York: Harper & Row, Publishers, Inc., 1980).

[2]George McGovern, "The New Right and the Old Paranoia," *Playboy* (January, 1981), p. 118. Copyright © 1980 by *Playboy*.

[3]*Ibid.*, p. 250.

Chapter 5

[1]Richard Quebedeaux, *The Worldly Evangelicals* (New York: Harper & Row, Publishers, Inc., 1978), p. 83.

[2]C. Norman Kraus, ed., *Evangelicalism and Anabaptism* (Scottdale, Pa.: Herald Press, 1979), p. 97.

[3]*Ibid.*, p. 83-100.

[4]John C. Cooper, *The Recovery of America* (Philadelphia: The Westminster Press, 1973).

[5]Kraus, *op. cit.*, pp. 99-100.

[6]*Toledo Blade* (November 16, 1980). Reprinted by permission from *The Blade*, Toledo, Ohio.

[7]Richard Kern, *John Winebrenner* (Harrisburg, Pa.: Central Publishing House, 1954).

[8]Johnny Greene, "The Astonishing Wrongs of the New Moral Right," *Playboy* (January, 1981), pp. 254-255. Copyright © 1980 by *Playboy*.

[9]George M. Marsden, *Fundamentalism and American Culture* (New York: Oxford University Press, 1980), p. 103.

[10]*Ibid.*, p. 189. See also Maynard Shipley, *War on Modern Science: A Short History of Fundamentalist Attacks on Evolution and Modernism* (New York: Alfred A. Knopf, Inc., 1927), pp. 3-4; Norman F. Furniss, *The Fundamentalist Controversy, 1919-1931* (New Haven, Conn.: Yale University Press, 1954), pp. 42-43, 57-70, 83-95; Richard Hofstadter, *The Paranoid Style in American Politics: And Other Essays* (Chicago: University of Chicago Press, 1963); "The Bible Crusaders' Challenge," *"The Crusaders' Champion Controversy I* (February 5, 1926, pp. 12-13, reprinted in Gatewood, ed., *Controversy*, pp. 243-247).

[11]Kenneth L. Woodward and Howard Fineman, *Newsweek* (September 15, 1980), p. 35.

[12]"A TV Preacher Sells America on Flag, Family and Freedom, of Sorts," *People* (December 29—January 5, 1981), pp. 60-61.

[13]Woodward and Fineman, *op. cit.*, p. 35.

[14]Greene, *op. cit.*, p. 260.

Chapter 6

[1]Karl R. Popper, *The Open Society and Its Enemies,* vols. 1 and 2 (Princeton, N. J.: Princeton University Press, 1950).
[2]Johnny Greene, "The Astonishing Wrongs of the New Moral Right," *Playboy* (January, 1981), p. 118. Copyright © 1980 by *Playboy.*
[3]Benito Mussolini, *The Doctrine of Fascism,* quoted in R.P. Wolff, *About Philosophy* (Englewood Cliffs, N. J.: Prentice-Hall, Inc., 1976), p. 136.
[4]*Ibid.,* p. 137.
[5]Greene, *op. cit.,* p. 258.
[6]Alan C. Elms, *Social Psychology and Social Relevance* (Boston: Little, Brown & Company, 1972).